A Handbook for Writing Formal Papers

FROM CONCEPT TO CONCLUSION

Fifth Edition

**Norman W. Steinaker
Terry A. Bustillos
National University**

Learning Solutions

New York   Boston   San Francisco
London   Toronto   Sydney   Tokyo   Singapore   Madrid
Mexico City   Munich   Paris   Cape Town   Hong Kong   Montreal

Pearson Learning Solutions, 501 Boylston Street, Suite 900, Boston, MA 02116
A Pearson Education Company
www.pearsoned.com

Printed in the United States of America

21   18

000200010270575621

KL

ISBN 10: 0-558-71358-0
ISBN 13: 978-0-558-71358-4

Table of Contents

In the formal writing process you need to be organized, thoughtful, and clear. Formal writing is a pristine exercise in clarity, continuity, and cogent thinking. There are five words or steps that can illuminate this writing process. They are define, describe, detail, discuss, and determine. These steps are intrinsic to the process of writing and to the organization, clarity, and thoughtfulness of your paper. They are the sequential steps that writers of formal papers follow. In the formal writing process these five sequential steps are the key to writing a successful paper that brings understanding and meaning to the reader. You need to be continually cognizant of them as you write your paper. Remember also that formal writing, while it has a style and character of its own as well as a particular format, should also be lively and interesting to the reader. The careful sequencing of these five steps in the development of your paper, done with craft and skill, can infuse liveliness and interest into your work. Again, the five words are define, describe, detail, discuss, and determine.

Define

The first obligation you have to the reader is to define the topic of your paper. Definition consists of a clear, concise, and coherent characterization of the nature of the topic being studied. This should be done in the first few paragraphs of your paper, preferably in the first paragraph. Let the reader know immediately the subject and focus of the paper, so there is a clear understanding of the purpose and what is to come in the paper. In defining the paper you should indicate the limits and parameters of the paper. It is essential that this be done early in the paper so the reader can quickly and clearly comprehend the topic as well as its focus and limitations. If you are writing a research proposal or research study you need to define the questions or issues you are addressing and how you have approached them. Through the clear and careful exposition of the topic and issues in your paper, the reader can make a decision as to how the content could be used for personal or professional purposes. Definition is the equivalent of memory and translation in the cognitive taxonomy and exposure in the experiential taxonomy (Steinaker & Bell, 1979).

 ## Describe

After the definition is clearly, concisely, and coherently stated, you will need to describe the topic so the reader understands the focus of your paper. You will need to provide, in the introduction or first section of your paper, some additional information to make it clear to the reader how you have limited and focused the topic of your paper. You will also need to establish the importance of the paper in the field. To do this you should provide the reader with a few salient citations and specifics about the topic. The reader should not only know what the topic is, but should have a clear understanding of why it is important. The reader should know, through the specific information you have provided, the importance of the topic and how it is to be focused and developed. You should also inform the reader why you have selected this topic. All of these elements describe your paper and give it substance, meaning, and purpose. When you have completed both the definition and the description, you have completed the introduction or first section of your paper. This describing process corresponds to translation and interpretation in the cognitive taxonomy and to participation in the experiential taxonomy.

 ## Detail

In the review of literature and method sections of the paper you detail or tell about what researchers, writers, and commentators have reported about the topic you have selected and how you have organized your study. It is your task to detail and inform for the reader, as objectively as possible, the information you have found through your reading and reviewing the literature. You simply relate the information without personal comment and without interpretation. You note, cite, and tell what has been done in the field and what you have discovered through your own review of literature. Nothing more is needed and nothing more should be done. You will need to organize your detailed information into headings and subheadings in the review of literature to clarify it, to explicate it, and to structure your paper for the reader. This kind of organization is always very helpful to the reader. You need to remember the review of literature provides the evidentiary basis for your discussion. When doing a research paper you will include a method section in which you detail the organization, the structure, and the process developed for your study. You will include information on data collection and analyses of these data. You must also include a results section in which you report your findings. These further add to your evidentiary base for your conclusions and your recommendations. You may utilize existing research models or you may develop a model specific to your study. The detail step in writing corresponds to the application and analysis levels of the cognitive taxonomy and the identification level of the experiential taxonomy.

 Discuss

This step in the formal writing process is done, and logically so, in the discussion section of your paper. If you are doing a review of literature only, this will be the final section of your paper. If you are doing a qualitative or quantitative study, this section will follow the method and results sections and will be the concluding section of your study. In a research study you will discuss not only the review of literature, but also your method and findings from the study. For review of literature papers you first summarize what you have found in the literature you reviewed. Then you interpret the literature usually, but not necessarily, by category. The elements you need to consider are as follows: You note consistencies and inconsistencies and you bridge the gaps. You compare and contrast. You construct and deconstruct. You identify the important and eliminate the non pertinent. You build your own perspective through this process. You let the reader know that you have understood, applied, and analyzed the information and the findings thoroughly and completely. Your discussion must be straight forward and professional. It must reflect the careful consideration you have given to the topic and the thoroughness of your review of literature. If you are doing an qualitative or quantitative study, this section follows the method and results section. You not only review the literature, but you incorporate the review with your method and your findings and bring them together in the discussion section of your study. This process in your paper corresponds to the analysis and synthesis levels of the cognitive taxonomy and to the internalization level of the experiential taxonomy.

Determine

In the final section of your paper you make determinations about the topic and what you have learned. Here you draw conclusions and make recommendations. These conclusions and recommendations should be consistent within the interpretation component of the discussion. They should reflect the summative evaluation of the literature you have reviewed, their correlation with the study, and the findings you have reported. These conclusions and recommendations should reflect the synthesis and evaluation levels of cognition. You should inform the reader why you have drawn your conclusions and why you have made your recommendations. The conclusions and recommendations should be stated clearly and succinctly. They are your final commentary on the topic and should summarize your thinking. Generate a succinct and strong statement of what you have thought, determined, concluded, and recommended in terms of the topic you have chosen and the study you have completed. Determining is consistent with the synthesis and evaluation levels of the cognitive taxonomy and the dissemination level of the experiential taxonomy.

Again, best wishes to you as you develop your paper. Make it important to you. Your readers will sense this and will react more positively to your work whether they agree with you or choose to disagree with you. Remember that your paper is a reflection of you and your professionalism. Make it the very best that it can be. In doing this you will have a product which will bring forth a sense of personal accomplishment.

In this course, as in many courses at your university or written expectations within your organization, you are expected to write a formal professional paper, a professional writing project, or a quantitative or qualitative study. For some of you this may be your first experience in writing a paper of this kind. For others this may be a further experience in writing. For all, this will be an opportunity to demonstrate your skills in writing. Writing a formal paper is a challenging task, but can be done well if you begin early in the course or time frame, keep to a personal schedule, and follow the style and format adopted by your university or your organization. This handbook has been prepared as a guide and a quick reference on how to organize your paper or your study. A section-by-section developmental format for writing your paper and a notation of some of the expectations of style and format that you will follow in preparing your paper have been included. You need to remember that the style manual for your paper is the latest edition of the *Publication Manual of the American Psychological Association* (APA). Your paper will consist of the following sections: Title page, abstract, introduction, review of literature, method, results, discussion, and references. Appendices and a bibliography, if you have them in your paper, will also be discussed. You should remember the method and results sections are included only for courses or papers requiring a quantitative or qualitative study. In some instances you may be asked to include a table of contents. The preparation of a table of contents is included as a part of this handbook in case it is expected or required.

If you are submitting a formal writing project or white paper, preparing a guidebook or handbook, planning a staff development program, evaluating a program, writing a grant proposal, doing an action research study, or preparing curriculum, you can learn how to prepare each of these in this work. We added these writing projects except one in the third edition. In the fourth edition we added how to prepare curriculum for those responsible for writing curriculum. This section on curriculum is designed both for teachers and for anyone designated to prepare curriculum for in services or for special training. We have added, in an appendix, a format for developing curriculum. You may use it or any other format suggested by your supervisor.

In this fifth edition of our work we have revised the work to include updated information consistent with the sixth edition of the *Publication Manual of the American Psychological Association*. There have been a number of changes from the fourth edition and we have detailed these in the chapters and sections relating to the development of the paper. In addition we have amended some of the material in the sections on common errors in writing formal papers and in formal writing conventions. Other parts of the document have been changed to make them consistent with the sixth edition of the *Manual*. We have also added for this edition two new sections. They are a section on preparing to write a personal response paper and a section on how to write papers, interaction with the instructor and peers, and doing assignments for online courses.

You have, in this work, directions on how to prepare each of these formal documents, proposals, programs, studies, curriculum, and writing papers and other material online. There are other kinds of papers you may need to prepare. You will find help in this work even though we may not discuss them in this work. The format for these other writing projects may vary somewhat, but they generally follow the formal writing style and format. We have provided a guide for writing formal papers that is functional and helpful for all kinds of formal writing. In this work, you have sections such as common errors, formal writing conventions, and a grammar usage section you can use for reference. The format and style for most of these other kinds of papers are frequently consistent with the APA. You will find that the APA format and style are discussed throughout this work. Consult your instructor or your supervisor for specific help in writing other kinds of formal writing projects.

Every professional graduate paper will contain some or all of the sections described in this *Handbook*. Instructors or supervisors may make minor adjustments in organization, but the basic component sections of the paper will be prepared as outlined in this *Handbook*. You need to remember every section of the paper begins at the top of a new page. In the new edition of the *Manual* this has changed in the method and results sections and that will be discussed in those sections. These notes are organized so expectations for each section of the paper are discussed sequentially. Writing tips are included at the end of the notes for each section of the paper. They are designed to help you focus on how to prepare the content of each section of your paper. In this fifth edition, we have included a model paper. You may use it as a reference for what a paper should look like. It is a model for a review of literature paper.

In the pages that follow, each section of the paper or study is discussed and described. There are differences between a quantitative or qualitative study and a review of literature paper and these differences are pointed out. Most papers written at the graduate level are reviews of literature. In only a few courses are papers requiring a research format expected. All elements of each section on a variety of formal papers and research studies are detailed in this work. Please be sure to refer to this work as you are writing your paper. You will be expected to adhere to the format and the writing style detailed in this work throughout your paper. In addition to the discussions about the sections of the paper, there are additional components of this work that you will need to review carefully.

The first component deals with common errors found in formal papers. If you study the nature of the errors and how to correct them when reviewing the preparation of the other sections of your work, you will be well on your way to writing a strong graduate or corporate paper, research study, or one of the programs discussed in this work. A second component in this work is a commentary on formal writing conventions. This commentary is provided to give you, as the writer, an additional perspective on writing formal papers. It is written in narrative form and provides another component and support for your writing. The third component is an end note with a focus on strategies for building your professional skills. In this fifth edition two additional sections have been added. They are section on preparing a personal response paper and a section on writing for online courses. Eight appendices are included that are keyed to sections the paper and formal writing conventions. In Appendix A, checklists for writing each section of the paper both for review of literature papers and for research studies is included including table of contents and bibliography. It is important that you use these checklists because they provide a list of the expectations and requirements for each section of the paper or study. Page number referents for finding information about each items on the checklist are noted for each item within the checklist for that section of the paper. Appendix B includes a suggested scoring rubric for formal papers. Appendix C is a suggested evaluation guide for formal papers. In Appendix D a format for presenting papers is provided. Appendix E contains a list of common references. Appendix F is a guide to developing surveys and questionnaires. Appendix G is a guide to formal grammar usage and has been augmented for this fifth edition. Appendix H is a format for planning curriculum. A glossary of terms pertaining to writing and research is included following the appendixes.

There are many additional sources for writing papers and research studies that can be used. Among them are the *Publication Manual of the American Psychological Association* (American Psychological Association, 2010), Cone and Foster's work (1993), Carver (1984), Strunk and White (2000), and Turabian (2007). If you are in the field of education and need general resources, consult Darling-Hammond (1997), Eisner (1994), Joyce and Weil with Calhoun (2004), and Reeves (2003). If you need additional resources in research use Gall, Borg, and Gall (1996), Mertens (2005), and Merriam (1998). There are, of course, many more. If you are in the business department you may wish to use, among others, Bennis (1997, 2000), Bennis and Goldsmith (2003), Drucker (1967), Howard (1993), Sample (2003), or Likert (1967). Again, there are many more resources for you to review and consult in these and other fields of study.

In this fifth edition a number of changes have been made. Additions and correction have been made in the explanations for how to do each section of the paper. These changes have been more substantive in the method and results sections of the work. Writing tips have been extended and are more detailed. There have been additions and changes made in the section on common errors in formal papers. Additional information has been included in the section on conventions of formal writing. In the sample references appendix, additional samples have been included for writer's use. The glossary has been extended to include more terms students and writers encounter in classes or in their organizations. We have added a section on preparing curriculum and have also included a model paper. We feel that, in this edition, the scope of the work has been broadened and the content, while remaining user friendly, has been expanded and made specific to the sixth edition of the *Publication Manual of the American Psychological Association.*. This fifth edition has been augmented by these additions and changes and has been reviewed for clarity, specificity, and necessary detail. Some of the changes we have made have come to us from students who have used the *Handbook*.

Suggestions have also come from our colleagues. We thank them for helping to make this edition one that writers will find even more useful than the first four editions.

We wish to acknowledge the assistance and support of our colleagues, our friends, and our students for reading and critiquing this work. Their assistance and responses have been invaluable as we have prepared this document. In field tests and in reviewing the document our students have been very helpful in asking questions, helping us clarify meaning and content, and in critiquing the *Handbook* as they used it. Special thanks go to the late John W. Stallings of the University of Southern California for his support and guidance early in the development of this work. We also want to thank James Mbuva of National University for his review of the manuscript and for his support in making it better and more complete. We want to thank Marilyn Koeller and Lorraine Leavitt, our colleagues, for their encouragement and help.

Especially, however, we want to thank our families. Their patience, their support and their love have meant much to us. Finally we want to thank the following: Dr. Natalia Bilan, Dr. Joseph R. Ruggio, and Dr. Richard A. Ott, without whom this work could not have been completed.

Abstract

The purpose of this work was to briefly explicate the format, organization, and style of formal papers for students. The *Publication Manual of the American Psychological Association* has been the format adopted by many universities and organizations. This work was consistent with that manual. It was designed as a guide for students and others when writing formal papers. Five steps in the process of writing a professional paper were included in the preface. Each section of the paper including title page, abstract, introduction, review of literature, method, results, discussion, references, and table of contents were addressed. Sections on how to prepare formal papers and white papers, guidebooks, staff development programs, program evaluation, grant proposals, action research, curriculum, personal responses, and writing for online courses have been included. Writing tips were included for each section. Conventions of formal writing were included. There were also discussions on common errors, grammar, and notes on building professional skills. Sections on grammar, writing formal papers, evaluating programs, writing funding proposals, and doing action research were also included. Checklists for each section were included in an appendix.

Preparing the Title Page

The title page is the first page of the paper and contains the following elements: Running head, title, author, and author's affiliation. Nothing more than this information needs to be included on the title page of the paper. If you are submitting a paper for publication, you may include the name of the department and an author's note. These elements are what the American Psychological Association manual requires. Be sure that the American Psychological Association (APA) style and format for this page are followed. If your professor, instructor, or supervisor has additional requirements, you should include them as part of your title page. The title page is always page one of your paper.

Page Header

It should be noted only that the page header is no longer used. It has been dropped in the sixth edition of the *Publication Manual* and has been replaced by the running head.

Running Head

The running head is placed on the top line of the title page. It is justified on the left margin. The *R* in running head is capitalized. The *h* in head is not capitalized. The words "Running head" are followed by a

> The title page is the first page of the paper and contains the following elements: Running head, title, author, and author's affiliation.

colon. Following the colon are the words within the running head. Those words are simply a short version of your full title not to exceed 50 characters, counting letters, punctuation, and spaces between words. The running head without the words "Running head" is used to head every page of your paper. The short version of the title in caps is justified on the left margin on every page. Justify the number to the right margin. "Use the automatic functions of your word-processing program to generate headers and page numbers for your file. (Do not type these manuscript page headers repeatedly in your word processing file" (Publication Manual, 2010, p. 230). There is a specific purpose for the running head. You are writing a professional paper that is suitable for publication. The running head you have selected tells the reviewer and the editor what you would like to use as the header for each page of your article or paper when it is published. This is also how your paper will be referred to in professional discussions and in some bibliographies and abstracts. The running head appears on all pages of your paper but without the word running head. The words "Running head" appear only on the title page. Use only the short version of the title all in caps plus the sequential page number justified to the right margin.

 ## Title

"The title should be typed in upper and lowercase letters, centered between the left and right margins, and positioned in the upper half of the page" (Publication Manual, 2010, p. 23). The recommended length of the title should be no more than 12 words. Avoid using acronyms or abbreviations in the title. Do not use italics or quotations in your title. Your title is a description of your paper or study. Make it clear and concise.

 ## Author

One double space below the title is your name. Your name is centered and justified with the title. Do not use the word by. For two authors, separate the names of the authors with the word and. Names should be placed on one line, space permitting. For three or more authors separate the names by a comma. Before the last author is listed use the word and. Authors' names, if necessary, can be placed on two or more lines with the names centered and justified under the title.

 ## Author's Affiliation

This is the department, university affiliation, or professional affiliation of the author. In most cases the affiliation will be the university in which you are enrolled or the organization of which you are a member. If you are submitting this paper for publication you may use the university, your school district, or your professional affiliation. The affiliation notation is centered one double space below the author's name. You can put the name of the department of the organization or the school to which you are assigned centered one double space below the affiliation.

Additional Information

In most instances no other information appears on the title page. Do not put course title, course number, instructor's name, or any other information on the title page unless required by the professor, the instructor, or your supervisor. If you are writing a research project for publication you may include an author note that includes each author's departmental information, and "provide [s] disclaimers or perceived conflict of interest, and provide a point of contact for interested readers" (*Publication Manual*, 2010, p. 24). An author's note does not apply to writers of papers, theses, or dissertations.

Writing Tips

Be sure to follow the format explicitly. The title page is the first page the reader examines. It should reflect the information needed. The page header is used no longer. It has been replaced by the running head. Select the running head carefully; it is a shorter version of your title. The running head is justified on the left margin. It is placed on the top line of the paper Do not use acronyms, italics, abbreviations, or quotation marks in your running head. Remember that the capitalized short version of the title is all in caps. It should not exceed fifty characters including spaces. Ensure that the title, your name, and your affiliation are centered at mid page. Count the spaces if necessary. Make the title of your paper clear, cogent, and concise.

For a quick review of all the required components of the title page refer to the checklist for the title page in Appendix A on page 125. The use of this checklist will ensure that you have included all the necessary components of the title page in your paper.

2

Preparing the Table of Contents

Chapter

A table of contents is not included in most formal papers because they tend to be relatively short. For longer papers and manuscripts such as this *Handbook*, a table of contents can be very helpful. A table of contents may also be required by your instructor or supervisor. Tables of contents are included immediately following the title page. Tables of contents are numbered in lower case Roman numerals as is the preface if one is included. Roman numerals are used only for the table of contents and any preface or other prefatory remarks. The introduction is also usually numbered in lower case Roman numerals.

Lower case Roman numerals, as noted, are used in the table of contents and are numbered one tab space following the running head short version of the title. The title of the section, table of contents, is centered one double space below the running head and is written in text. The name of each section or chapter of the work is entered on a line beginning one double space below the table of contents title. A dotted line with one space between each dot completes the line to the page number that is justified on the right. Each succeeding section is listed one double space below the preceding section. When headings are included, they must be indented one tab space on the line below the section title. There must be at least two headings when they are listed. This pattern continues until all sections and heading information are noted by page numbers. Titles of chapters, sections, headings, and subheadings are written in text, not bold.

> *Tables of contents are included immediately following the title page.*

Page numbers are provided for each chapter, section, heading, and heading. The page numbers are justified on the right margin. If your paper has subheading, they are indented one tab space below the chapter or section heading. A second level of headings is indented two tab spaces from the left margin or one tab space more than headings. If you have headings or subheadings in your table of contents there must be at least two of each. In the *Publication Manual* (2010) there are five levels of headings (page 62). Headings and subheadings are discussed in the chapter on the review of literature. See the table of contents for this document as an example of how to prepare your table of contents. Appendixes are listed in the table of contents.

Writing Tips

Preparing a table of contents must be done accurately and carefully. Be sure that you have one space between each dot on the line from the end of the title of that section, category, or subcategory to the number of the page. Remember that page numbers are justified on the right margin. Use Arabic numbers only, except for the notation of the preface and other prefatory materials. Categories are indented one tab space and are entered on the line below the section or chapter title. There must be at least two category titles when they are used. If you have subcategories, they are indented and entered two double spaces from the left margin or one tab space more than categories. There must be at least two subcategory titles entered when they are used. Just a word on prefaces and prefatory remarks; prefaces are not included in short papers or research studies and if they are, they serve to introduce the work, to illustrate its organization, and to acknowledge those who assisted you and supported you during the development of the work. Do not include any prefatory comments unless specifically asked to do so by your instructor or supervisor.

For a quick review of the expected elements of the table of contents, refer to the checklist in Appendix A (page 126). The use of this checklist will help ensure that you have completed the required components and format for the table of contents.

3 Preparing the Abstract

Chapter

The abstract is page two of your paper. An abstract, as a model, is included on page xvii of this work. The abstract has a running head and is numbered as page two of the paper. One double space below the running head is the word abstract which is centered. The a in abstract is capitalized, none of the other letters in the word is capitalized. The word abstract is written in bold. The purpose of the abstract is to inform the reader very succinctly about the purpose of your paper, the parameters of the topic included in the paper, and the pertinence or importance of the paper in the field. You should also note salient points you have found in your review of literature. If you have written a research study you will state the problem or question you investigated as part or all of the purpose of the paper. Your findings, conclusions, and recommendations are also included. Readers will choose to read your paper or not to read your paper based on what you include in the abstract. The abstract thus becomes the most important part of your paper in terms of how many people read your paper. It must be very carefully written.

The APA indicates that the word count in the abstract is typically between 150 and 250 words. For shorter papers and online writing some instances instructors or supervisors may allow you up to 150 words. The abstract is written as one narrative paragraph. "A well prepared abstract may be the most important single paragraph" (*Publication Manual*, 2010, p. 26) in your

> The purpose of the abstract is to inform the reader very succinctly about the purpose of your paper, the parameters of the topic included in the paper, and the pertinence or importance of the paper in the field.

paper. Readers are interested in a quick concise overview of your paper. Any additional words could deter from the purpose of the abstract which is to inform reviewers and readers and to cause them to be interested in your work. In order to conserve words, use no citations or quotations and be as succinct as possible. An abstract should be coherent and readable. At the same time, however, be very specific about the purpose, salient points, content, conclusions, and recommendations of your paper.

The abstract is not indented. It is blocked. It consists of one paragraph with all lines justified only on the left margin of the paper. Right margins are not justified in the abstract, nor are they justified on the right margin anywhere in the paper except for the page numbers in the table of contents. The narrative of the paragraph begins one double space below the word abstract. All narrative lines are double-spaced. Do not break words at the end of a line. No line should end with a hyphen. A good abstract is accurate, concise, and specific. You report what the paper was about and include in the abstract salient points from your review of literature, your findings, your conclusions, and your recommendations. The abstract is not evaluative. No personal opinions or statements can or should be included. The conclusions and recommendations which should be included in the abstract are the nearest you can come to expressing your ideas or perspectives and even these should retain a non-evaluative tenor.

Abstracts are written in the past or present perfect tense. The opening sentences define the purpose of the paper or the issues studied in your paper. These sentences identify the parameters and limitations of the paper and its importance to the field. The next few sentences emphasize the major points from the review of literature as well as notations on your method and your findings if you have done a research study. In the last few sentences of the abstract summarize your findings, your conclusions and recommendations.

The abstract is the last section of the paper that is written. You usually complete the introduction, review of literature, the method, the results, and the discussion sections before writing the abstract. Once you have completed the paper and clearly understand the scope, sequence, and findings of your work, you can then write the abstract with more clarity, precision, and focus. Write clearly and concisely using simple sentences so that the reader can quickly gain insight into the topic of your paper, its purpose, its parameters, what you learned about the topic, your findings, and your conclusions and recommendations. Avoid citations in the abstract because they count as words and thus decrease the number of words you can use to tell the reader what needs to be understood about the paper.

When your paper has been published the abstract may appear as the initial introduction or paragraph of your paper in the journal of publication. It may or may not be noted as the abstract. Abstracts are also published in various professional publications such as Educational Resources Information Center (ERIC) and APA Psychological Abstracts.

Writing Tips

Be sure to keep to the word limitation of 150 to 250 words. In shorter papers the expected number of words may be fewer. Your abstract is written in the past and/or present perfect tense. Eliminate any unnecessary words or phrases. Use short simple sentences as much as possible. Do not use acronyms in the abstract. Avoid using adjectives and adverbs as much as possible. Use technical terms and language only if they are absolutely necessary. Do not include citations or resources. Your abstract should be non evaluative and should be concise, coherent, and readable. It should be clear and easy to read. Remember to include conclusions and recommendations. These are generally included in the last sentence or sentences of the abstract. In a research study you should include the question or issue you studied. You need to note whether your study was a quantitative or qualitative study or a combinations of both major kinds of studies. You will also, in a research study, need to include a summary statement of the findings or the results of your study. There should be no personal bias within the abstract.

For a quick review of the expected elements of the abstract refer to the checklist for abstracts in Appendix A on page 127. The use of this checklist will help ensure that you have included all expected components of the abstract in your paper.

Preparing the Introduction

Chapter

The introduction is the first narrative section of your paper. It is noted on the page header as page three of your paper. You center the full title of your paper one double space below the running head. If you need two lines for the title of your paper use them. Be sure the second line of the title is centered one double space below the first line of the title. All first letters in the words of the title are capitalized except for articles and prepositions. Do not title this section introduction.

In the introduction there are three basic components. First, you define the purpose of the paper. If you are writing a research study you need to include in your purpose the question or issue you are studying. You will also, for research studies state succintly how your study relates to other studies in the area. You will also need to note the theoretical and practical implications of the study. Second, you establish the importance of the topic in the field of study. You include citations and short quotes as necessary to verity the importance of the topic. Third, you provide a rationale for choosing the topic and for your interest in the topic. Nothing more is necessary for inclusion in the introduction.

Purpose of Paper

In defining the purpose of your paper you provide only as much information as is necessary. The purpose or purposes can be written in a few sentences or, depending

> Your reader should understand the purpose of the paper, why it is important, and why you have an interest in the topic.

on the topic, can be slightly longer. Make sure the reader has a clear understanding of the purpose of the paper, how you have defined it, and its limitations. If your problem or topic has many components or facets you will need to define the parameters of your paper carefully and make sure that the focus is clearly stated and specific. You may also include the issue or question being reviewed or studied. The reader needs to understand the purpose at the beginning of the paper. Make your purpose clear and provide as much information as you need in order to provide the reader with a clear and concise presentation of your purpose in writing the paper. If you are preparing a quantitative or qualitative study, you will need to clearly define the question or the issue and the variables being studied in the purpose of your research. You will need to note how your study relates to recent other studies in the field and state any secondary hypotheses as well as the objectives of the study. You may also need to include some information on population and process as well as on data collection instruments and how they were evaluated. This information must be briefly stated and provide enough information for the reader to clearly understand the focus, limitations, and parameters of the study. In writing your statement of purpose, you need to make it concise, clear, and cogent and provide as much information you feel the reader needs. In many instances you are writing within a specified time frame or deadline so your topic or purpose must be something you can develop well within the time frame under which you are working. Your first paragraph or few paragraphs of the introduction should make the purpose of the paper clear to the reader and provide the reader with a focused purpose for the paper as well as its parameters and limitations.

 ## Importance of Topic

After you have written your purpose statement, you have the obligation to emphasize the importance of the topic. Remember that the work you are preparing is a professional paper or research study and needs to evidence a substantive contribution to the field. In this component of the introduction you will briefly bring forward issues that will be reviewed in your paper and develop a background for the reader so that the topic and the issues within it are recognized as important to the profession. This background of information should be defined and prepared with clarity and with evidence to support it. You should discuss briefly the literature you have reviewed and cite only salient points from your review. You do not go into great detail in the introduction because you will do this in your review of literature. In the introduction you are defining and describing, not going into detail. Your review of literature will be organized around categories and subcategories of your topic and will provide the detail needed. You may want to organize this part of the introduction around those categories, though this is not mandatory nor is it essential in establishing the importance of the topic. You will need to use some citations, even several, in this section. You must establish the importance of the topic through evidence from sources. Do not go into an exhaustive review of literature in the introduction. As the writer you cannot establish the importance of the topic. The importance can only be established by the sources, authors, commentators, and researchers you cite. You may also use internet resources. Use only pertinent and seminal sources that emphasize the importance of the topic, the question, or the issues. Do only enough so that the reader understands the importance of the topic and has a good grasp of the background of the topic as well as the limitations and parameters of the paper. The reader should know not only the subject of the paper and its importance, but also know the specific issues and topics that are the focus of your paper as well as some of the resources you discuss within the review of literature. In research studies you will need to cite current and recent studies that illustrate research pertaining to your topic, thus illustrating the importance of the topic.

Rationale for Choosing Topic

To provide closure in the introduction you will want to identify the rationale or your reason for selecting this topic. Let the reader know why you are doing the paper or the study and why you have an interest in the issues or questions discussed in your paper or your study. Your choice can come from a personal need to learn more about the topic. It can come from a feeling that exploring the area and studying it will help you and your colleagues become professionally more competent. Your choice can also be made because this topic has within it issues that are pertinent to your school, your district, company, corporation or workplace. The rationale for a research study could be the need to test a theory, an intervention, or to determine attitudes and perspectives about an issue or a problem. Your rationale could be to test a theory, issue, variable, or intervention with a different population. There could also be other professional reasons. You define your reasons and state them succinctly and to the point. Do not go into great detail. Completing the rationale closes the introduction.

Writing Tips

It is important to remember to write the introduction in a non-evaluative style. You do not reveal any biases, predetermined expectations, or outcomes at this point in the paper. Your writing should reflect your professional interest in the topic and a recognition that the topic is important to you and to the profession or organization. Everything in this section should be written in the past tense and/or present perfect tense except for direct quotes. This is very important and you should review what you have written to correct any tense as well as other syntactic issues. One of the most common errors for those who are just beginning the process of writing formal papers is syntax. Avoid compound and complex sentences as much as possible though they may occasionally be necessary. About eighty percent or more of your sentences should be simple declarative sentences. Write clearly and use short simple sentences consistently to ensure clarity, cogency, and continuity. Say only what needs to be said and use an economy of expression. Keep in mind that "brevity is the soul of wit." William Shakespeare was correct. You can write with clarity, cogency, and develop continuity through saying only what needs to be said briefly. In doing this you can effectively retain interest and involvement by the reader. Your reader should understand the purpose of the paper or study, why it is important, and why you have an interest in the topic. This is most important and you need to ensure that these are included in the paper. Sometimes writers include a transitional paragraph after the three components have been finished. While this is not necessary, it can give the reader an understanding of what is coming next in the paper and how the remaining sections are organized. This paragraph, if it is included, is generally brief, but may help the reader make a smooth transition from the introduction to the review of literature and a clear picture of how you have organized the paper. Finally, do not use superscript or subscript in your paper unless they are used for a scientific or mathematical formula or is approved for usage by the APA.

For a quick review of the expected elements of the introduction refer to the checklist for the introduction in Appendix A on page 128. The use of this checklist will help you ensure that you have included all the necessary components for the introduction of your paper.

5 Preparing the Review of Literature

Chapter

This section of your paper or study follows the introduction and is called the review of literature. This section is a major professional component of your paper. It is often the longest section of your paper or study. The review of literature also provides the foundation for information and commentary about your topic. It is titled review of literature. The review of literature begins on a separate page with the title centered one double space below the running head. As noted, the review of literature is almost always the longest and most detailed section of your paper or study. It is designed to informs the reader about the literature you have reviewed. It provides your report on the issues and content of the literature reviewed. The review of literature includes only sources that are pertinent to your paper. Your review of literature also provides an evidentiary base for your conclusions and recommendations in a review of literature paper. If you are writing a quantitative or qualitative research study, the review of literature not only provides an evidentiary base for the question or issue you are studying or testing. In addition, the review of literature provides the reader with a review of concurrent and corollary research in the field. The review of literature is generally organized with an introductory paragraph, categories delineating major areas of focus within the review, and sometimes with subcategories within the broader categories. The introductory paragraph serves as an organizational

> *The review of literature is generally organized with an introductory paragraph, categories delineating major areas of focus within the review, and sometimes with subcategories within the broader categories.*

content design for your paper and should be brief and clearly written. In some instances a closing paragraph may be included, even though it is not generally necessary in most papers.

 ## Introductory Paragraph

The introductory paragraph of the review of literature is generally relatively brief and contains only information about how the review of literature is organized. You will name the Level two headings and level three subheadings in the sequence in which they appear in the review of literature. Names of levels of level two headings are capitalized except for articles. Names of levels or headings are not capitalized unless they are the first word proper nouns. If you include level two headings and level three headings, you will name the level two heading and then the level three headings immediately following the naming of the level two section heading. Level three headings are necessary when they help you focus on specific information within a level two heading section of the review of literature. There must be at least two level two heading sections within the paper. Likewise, there must be at least two level three subheadings within each level two heading where they are used. The names of the level two and level three headings should be brief; usually one or two words and seldom more than three or four words. In a qualitative or quantitative study, you will follow the same content guidelines for your introductory paragraph. The level two and level three headings or sections should relate directly to research in the area of study as well as to related and corollary studies pertinent to your own research. Do not provide any other information in the introductory paragraph. The sole purpose of the paragraph is to inform the reader about the organization of the review of literature. It is, in a sense, a table of contents for the review of literature. Immediately following the opening paragraph, the title of the first level two heading section is provided. The title of each level two heading section is on a separate line, is justified on the left margin, and is in bold.

The APA identifies five levels of headings. In formal papers, generally only three are used. The highest level of heading or level one headings are called the titlecase headings and are used to head the sections of your paper. It is centered one double space below the running head. All title headings are in bold except the title page, the abstract, the introduction, references, and appendices.

 ## Level Two Headings

The second level of heading or major section in your review of literature helps you organize your review into logical areas of focus and that are defined areas of emphasis.

They are justified to the left margin, are in bold, and have upper case and lower case wording. Only articles are not capitalized. Using heading sections helps the writer organize findings and information for the review in terms of identified components of the paper as noted in the purpose of the paper and stated in the introduction. Heading sections also help the reader to focus on specific information related to the content of the level two headings. Each category needs to relate to the purpose of the paper or study as you have defined it in the introduction. The name of each second level heading section is on a separate line and is written in bold one double space below the narrative line above. Every word in the level two heading sections is capitalized except for articles and prepositions. The name of the level two heading is justified on the left margin. The narrative begins on the next line.

When writing about the literature reviewed, you must be objective. No personal opinions, biases, or interpretations can be expressed in the review of literature. Your review of literature must be non-evaluative. Avoid using value words or words that can be misinterpreted when writing the review of literature. Let the researchers, the authors, and commentators speak for themselves. You can paraphrase their works and use direct quotes, but you do not interpret them or comment on them. Paraphrases need to be cited. Your comments are reserved for the interpretation component of the discussion section of your paper. You should write the review of literature in the past tense and/or the present perfect tense with the exception of direct quotes where the author may use the present or future tense. Remember every resource you have reviewed has already been written and published in some context. If there are differing views among the researchers or writers within a particular category you should indicate this, but without personal comment or interpretation. Direct quotes require citations and page numbers. Use parentheses before and after direct quotes under forty words. Quotes of forty or more words must be blocked. To block a quotation, indent every line of the quotation one tab space. Do not use quotation marks for quotes of forty or more words. All blocked quotes are double spaced. If you paraphrase a researcher's or author's work, you must provide a citation. Indeed, every time you bring new information to the attention of the reader there must be a citation. Every paragraph including new information must have one or more citations. You must follow APA style and format or some other approved style and format for all citations.

You should go into as much detail as necessary when you are reviewing an article, a book, a document, internet material, visual material, or other resources. Through the material you have reviewed you are presenting information about the topic for the reader and providing an evidentiary basis for your interpretation, findings, conclusions, and recommendations. These become part of the discussion section of the paper. You are also demonstrating the importance of your sources in the field and their relationship to the paper or to the study. You need to provide for the reader evidence of a clear understanding of how the resources relate to the level two heading content in which they are cited. How the resources relate to the topic and to what the authors presented in their articles, books, or studies are essential. It is important that the citations and quotations be consistent in content with the context of the level two headings and the topic. In the review of literature you provide the reader with the information you have determined to be pertinent in explicating the issues, questions, or problems you have defined as the focus and purpose of your paper or study. In each heading you provide evidence from sources most closely related to the content of that level two heading.

 ## Level Three Headings

Level three headings or subsections are component parts of a level two heading. You must have at least two level three subheadings in each level two headings to justify their use. Subheading sections provide for more specific areas of focus or component parts of the second level heading in which they appear. You have more organizational flexibility when you use level three subheadings. For example, if your level three two heading is about teaching strategies, in the content of each level three section you can focus on one or more of the identified strategies chosen for review. Level three headings follow the same organization and writing style as categories. Titles of level three headings should be no more than two or three words. The title of each level three heading is written in bold. The third level heading is indented one tab space and is followed by a period. The narrative begins immediately following the title of the level three heading on the same line as the title of the level three heading. Only the first word of the level three headings and proper nouns are capitalized.

 ## Closing Paragraph

A closing paragraph is infrequently included, but if your review is lengthy or you wish to recapitulate the organization, you can include this paragraph. The only purpose of this paragraph is to again remind the reader what you have done in the review of literature. You simply rename the second level sections and third level subsections to remind the reader what you have included in your review of literature. You do not introduce new information or use citations. You write your closing paragraph without personal commentary or interpretation. That is reserved for the discussion section of the paper. In most instances this paragraph is not needed, but if you feel the need to include it, please do so.

Writing Tips

The review of literature is usually the longest section of your paper. It is written in narrative form and must follow the APA format and style. Clarity of expression and logical continuity are important elements of writing. Use an economy of expression. Say only what needs to be said. Use simple sentences most of the time. Compound and complex sentences should be avoided, unless needed for explanation or clarification. Avoid the use of jargon, buzz words, and overuse of professional terminology. Do not use colloquialisms, idioms, or slang expressions in your paper. You are writing a formal paper. You are writing for an audience of your peers and they read the paper with similar professional backgrounds and experiences.

Your review of literature should be written in the past and/or present perfect tense except for direct quotes. Whenever you introduce new information to the reader, you must cite the source of that information. If you use a direct quote, you must cite the source and the page number. Use quotation marks at the beginning and end of direct quotes of less than forty words. Direct quotes of forty or more words must be blocked. You do not use quotation marks with blocked quotes. If a blocked quote has a quotation within it, use a single quotation mark (apostrophe) before and after that quote within a quote. show that quotation. Do not use superscript or subscript except in certain mathematical or scientific formulae as defined within the APA *Manual*. You should predominantly use the active voice in your writing. Be very careful to eliminate any anthropomorphisms. We have found that to be one of the most common problems in writing. Check the grammar section of this work for more information on anthropomorphisms. Remember that research cannot tell nor report, neither can articles or books say. Only researchers and authors can tell, report, write, or say. Even in this day of political correctness, there should be agreement of subject and verb as well as in the use of personal pronouns. Avoid the use of he/she even though in a very few cases it may be unavoidable. Sentences, if they are well crafted, can for the most part, be written without using he/she. Make sure the reader understands the referent when you use a personal pronoun. When referring to people use who or whom. When referring to animals or inanimate objects use that or which. While there are certain well defined conventions for formal writing, they must be followed. At the same time you should strive to make your paper lively and interesting to the reader. Simplicity and continuity create a more fluent paper where meaning is more easily understood. You can go into as much detail as is necessary through a simple, straightforward, cogent style. Remember that you need to identify relations, contradictions, differences of opinion, gaps, and inconsistencies in the literature review. Strive to make your review of literature reflect these kinds of focus. Be sure there is a sound and sequential narrative flow. Be sure also to edit and carefully review this section of your paper or study. This is important in order to make sure that your review of literature is consistent with the purpose of your paper. You need to provide in your review of literature an evidentiary base for your conclusions and recommendations. The review of literature should also reflect the content necessary to ensure that the reader clearly understands the scope and sequence of the resources you have reviewed and how they pertain to your topic. Be sure that everything in the review of literature is double-spaced.

For a review of the elements necessary to the review of literature refer to the checklist for the review of literature in Appendix A on page 129. The use of the checklist will ensure that you have included all the components essential for a review of literature in your paper or study.

6

Preparing the Method Section

Chapter

A method section is included only in papers when you are doing a qualitative or quantitative research study. In a research study the method section immediately follows the review of literature. Almost all other formal papers are referred to as review of literature papers. Some undergraduate and graduate classes require a research study. Research studies are used in companies, foundations, and corporations as well. The method section describes in detail how the study was conducted. If you are doing a research study and need to include a method section you need to include all or most of the following categories or subsections: Question or issue being studied, limitations of the study, variables, population, sample size, time frame, process, data collection, data analysis, and assessment and evaluation. For some specific studies there may be other categories. In some instances there may be some redundancy, but in each category there is a defined focus with the need to present the information from a specific perspective. Research studies can be either quantitative or qualitative. The title method is one double space below the running head.

Quantitative studies are experimental, empirical, positivist and statistical. The focus of quantitative studies is on prediction, attitudes and perceptions, confirmation, and the testing of interventions or hypotheses. The analysis is deductive and the findings are precise and numerical. Qualitative studies focus on the nature and the essence of groups of people. They involve case studies, fieldwork, ethnography, and

> *A method section is included only in papers when you are doing a qualitative or quantitative research study.*

phenomenology. The goal of a qualitative investigation is understanding the beliefs and attitudes of a group, the structure of identified phenomena, constructivist methodology, and generating grounded theory. The mode of analysis is inductive and the findings are comprehensive and richly descriptive.

You need to determine which of these approaches to research would be more appropriate for your study. In some instances a study could include both kinds of research approaches. Each of the components or sections in a research study is shown below with a brief description of the content that should be included in each category. They are shown in the context of level two headings. The title of each category or section is written in bold and is on a separate line from the text as shown below.

Question or Issue

The questions or issues you are studying are the core purposes of your paper. You stated them as part of the purpose in the introduction to your paper and you need to restate them at the very beginning of your method section. In this section of the paper you need to clarify for the reader the issues and questions motivating the study as well as specific variables being examined and tested. You delimit the area of study within the identified questions or issues noted. You need to be very specific here so that the reader clearly understands what you are studying and how you have focused your particular study. These initial statements of the question or issue are key to the method section of your paper and need to be very carefully done. In this category or section of the method section you are delimiting the scope of the paper and defining its parameters. Craft it so there is no ambiguity about what your questions or issues are and how you are framing them. You also need to note the specific focus of the study. You are stating the purpose of the research, the questions or issues studied, and the variables tested. You are also defining, in this section the limitations of the study. You may list briefly other studies in the same area. You may need also to include briefly some information on the population, measures used, process, and analyses of the date even though these will be more fully developed later. Here they simply provide a very brief overview of the study and are included for clarity of understanding the nature of the study.

Limitations

There has never been a study that is totally complete and without flaw. Every research study has limitations and defined parameters. You need to point out some of those limitations in the study you are doing. Among those limitations could be the size of the population and whether they volunteered, were a convenience sample, or were selected at random. Limitations could also be areas of information or the variables that you are studying or those variables that you are not studying. Limitations can be the time frame for completing the study. The definition of limitations help the reader understand what you are not including in the study and what the constraints of the study imply for your work. Limitations can also be resources, funds, and materials available. Limitations could further include the kind of instruments selected for gathering and analyzing data. Other limitations could include variables studied, resources, and personnel. In this section you need to make clear to the reader how each of these limitations affected the study or related to the outcomes.

 ## Variables

In any research paper there are many variables that could be studied. The demographic data gathered in a survey, questionnaire, or interview can help you identify the variables in qualitative studies. An intervention or a treatment to be used with a group can constitute a variable. In this category of the method section you list the variables you plan to test in the study. You may also note some variables you are not testing. Variable definition is exceptionally important both to you and to your readers. Each component element you are testing or studying could be a variable. You need to know and your readers need to know very specifically and definitionally the variables that are being studied and tested within the study. The definition of variables should provide, for the reader, a clear and concise statement of what you are studying or what you are testing. Some research studies fail because the variables tested are not clearly defined. Variables should have a clearly defined and direct relationship to the purpose of the study. Sometimes you may be working with only one variable, but often two or more variables are involved in the study. You may want to focus on the expected outcomes for the identified variables and interpret the projected outcomes for their impact on the population. If you do this, the variables need to be noted. You will provide details and interpretation in the results and discussion sections of the study. You can also note related variables not included in the study. You need to include all these items in the variable category of your method section.

 ## Population

Who you are studying is also very important. You identify the population studied in this component of the method section. Populations vary in terms of the kind of study in which you are involved. Quantitative studies usually, but not always, require both a control and experimental group. These two groups need to be as equally matched as possible. Quantitative studies can also include a population responding to surveys, questionnaires, or interviews. Qualitative studies generally require only one group. Population size can vary according to the nature of the study. If you are doing a single case study your population is one person. If you are doing a large quantitative study your population could be hundreds or even thousands. If you are doing a lengthy or longitudinal study, you need to account for an attrition of members of the identified population. You must define age group, characteristics, gender, commonalities, and differences. You need to provide the reader information on how you selected the population and why they were selected. Note whether they were selected randomly or were a convenience population. Note any criteria used for selection of the population. These criteria could be experience, achievement, specific skills, or other identified personality or behavioral attributes. Do this notation clearly and succinctly for your readers. Make sure the readers clearly understand how the population was selected, why it was selected, and the criteria used for their selection. It is important for your readers to know this if they wish to replicate the study.

You must, here or in a general statement preceding the categories, ensure that ethical compliances have been met. The research study should be approved by an Institutional Review Board of the university or institution through which the study is approved and completed. If humans are used in the study, the researcher is responsible for making sure that the research design is clear and appropriate to the discipline. The assurance that the selection of subjects is fair, and that subjects are informed as to how they were selected must be done. Voluntary participation must be made explicit. Informal consent procedures are appropriate for the subjects. Informed consent procedures should be appropriate for the subjects. Protection of privacy and/or confidentiality is adequate to the study. Potential risks are identified and mitigated. It must be asured that the benefits of the research outweigh the risks. Finally a letter of consent and research instruments are attached to the proposal before the Institutional Review Board.

Sampling Process

This could be a separate category in the method section of your study, or it could be included within the population category subsection. You may break this out as a separate section if you need to describe in detail your sampling strategies and procedures. Here you need to provide a rationale for the size of the population, how the population is selected, and why it is limited to the particular size you chose. You may need to justify the size of the population in terms of why it is not larger or smaller. Sample size information could also include details about any subgroups within the population and how they might relate to variables being tested. You may also need to note the kind of sampling techniques used in selecting your population. You may, for example, need to note variances in achievement, experience, or skills as being subgroups in the population. The use of sample size as a separate subcategory or subsection in the method section of the paper allows you to do a more detailed description of the nature of the population in terms of subgroups within it and in terms of variables tested. You need to note how you chose your sample. Note whether it was a random selection or a convenience sample. Other sampling strategies used also need to be addressed in this category. This kind of information could also help frame the selection and definition of the variables studied.

 ## Time Frame

Here you simply provide the reader with the time frame for the study. Within this time frame you may want to note the sequence of activities and events in the study such as pre and post tests, as well as points of emphasis and benchmarks at specific times during the study. The category on the time frame can include information such as when and how data are collected, when data are analyzed, and when the final report of the study will be ready for presentation or publication. A time frame is not only the beginning time and ending time, it is a catalogue and sequence of activities and events within the time frame. Any funds should be keyed to components within the time frame. The time frame will help keep you on task and oriented toward an appropriate sequence of activities within the time frame. It will also keep the reader informed about the time sequence in which the study was done and the activities and events involved therein. If the reader wishes to replicate the study, the specifics of the time frame can be very helpful.

 ## Process

In this component or subsection of the method section you tell the reader how you did the study. You list the steps and sequence of activities. In a quantitative study you note the pre and posttests and the nature of the intervention or treatment. In a qualitative study you note your observations, interviews and review of documents. You indicate how you coded the data from them. For both kinds of research study you explain the process in a step-by-step sequential manner. You need to be careful to note each of the sequential steps and discuss each step briefly. If you expect problems with at any activity or step within the process, be sure to mention them. Your purpose in this part of the method section is to delineate the formative process and make it clear to the reader. In effect, this is a brief overview of the study and how it was accomplished.

This category of the method section can also include brief statements about how the data were gathered, analyzed, and evaluated. A more explicit discussion of these topics comes later in the method section, but for the reader to understand the process, you will want to briefly note them.

In any study there are formative processes and summative processes. The formative process is as important as the summative findings of the study if the study is to be replicated or the findings implemented. In this category of the method section your direct focus on the formative process. You need to relate the formative process to the summative outcomes briefly in this category of the method section of the paper. When the readers finish this category of the method section of the paper, they should have a clear understanding of how you completed the study, the steps within the process, issues and problems within the steps, and the linkage of that process to the summative outcomes.

Data Collection

How you collect the data is essential information for the reader. You need to include, in this category, information on the instruments you used in your study. You need to tell about the tests, questionnaires, observations, surveys, interviews, document reviews, and any other measures you used to gather data on your population and on the variables tested. Instruments and other measures used need to be described and made clear to the reader. These measures will be different in qualitative and quantitative studies. In qualitative studies the researcher is the primary instrument. You generally use interviews, observations, and document reviews including historical documents. The researcher needs to explain how you coded the responses in terms of the variables studied. In many cases these responses will be in coded narrative form. In quantitative studies you use tests, scales, surveys, questionnaires, completion of projects, or reports. Some studies combine both kinds of research. If you wish your readers to see your instruments or measures in their totality, they can be included in an appendix. Your obligation in the method section of the paper is to ensure that the reader understands what measures you used and how you gathered the information. The process of data collection needs to be clearly stated. You may need to comment on how it was categorized and stored. You may need to establish the validity and reliability of your measures if they are expected or required. This is particularly necessary if you have developed your own instruments and if you are doing a quantitative study.

Data Analysis

Your task in this part of the method section is to define the methods, measures, and processes used to analyze the data you have collected. If you are doing a quantitative study or are involved in an experimental, empirical, and statistical study, you will be using scales, tests, surveys, and questionnaires for gathering your data. You need to define the statistical analyses used whether they be descriptive statistical measures, correlational statistical measures, inferential statistical measures, or a combination of these statistical measures. If you are using descriptive statistical analyses you may be using mean, median, mode, average mean gain, range, and standard deviation. If you are using inferential statistical measures the most commonly used are the t test and chi square to measure for significance although there are many other inferential measures. You may use the Pearson r or other measures for correlational analyses. There are many statistical measures available for analysis of data. You need to select those most appropriate for your study.

If you are doing a qualitative study, you are focusing on the nature or essence of the population in terms of the variables tested. You need to identify how you coded materials gathered data, identified recurrent patterns, commonalities, and differences, including how you analyzed and examined those data and generalizations. This is usually done in a detailed narrative form in qualitative studies. You will, in addition, need to relate how the study evolved during its duration. You will need to determine if any grounded or substantive theory emerged from the study. You, as the researcher, are the primary instrument in data collection. These are the expectations your reader can have in this part of the method section in qualitative studies.

 ## Assessment and Evaluation

You have finished your category on data analysis. In terms of assessment and evaluation you take into consideration the formative and summative results of the study. You discuss them in terms of their generalizability, their replication, and their application to other similar populations or even different populations. You must also note what the assessment and evaluation mean. You may also need to address how the final report will be prepared and to whom it is to be addressed and distributed. The researcher has the obligation in this part of the method section to bring the process together in a final statement about the study and what it means. You need here to describe both the formative and summative processes in terms of how the study progressed and what the issues and problems were that arose during the process. This is particularly important for qualitative studies and needs to be included in the narrative. The assessment and evaluation component is not a statement of findings, but is your final statement about the study itself. It is the summary of the process both formative and summative of how you arrived at your findings. It provides a basis for the coming conclusions and recommendations.

Writing Tips

The writing style of the method section is the same as it is in the other sections of your study. You seek for clarity and a cogent presentation of the narrative. You need to include enough detail so that the reader clearly understands the content of each of the categories. You should also remember that everything in the method section is written in the past tense or in the present perfect tense. This section is more technical in some respects than the introduction and review of literature and you should pay close attention to the information you present and how you present it. This section usually contains terminology that is specific to the study and statistical terms that are not always reader friendly. You should, therefore, write in simple sentences with an economy of expression, carefully wrought syntax, and with a studied clarity. Verbosity, as you know, is the last refuge of mediocrity. You are writing for your peers, but even so, you may need to explain some terms that are specific to your study. You will also be using more professional terminology in this section than in the previous sections. Make sure the technical terminology is in context and is made as clear as possible to the reader. Some of your categories in this method section may be relatively brief. Make sure, however, that all the information needed is presented in a sequential and logical manner. Your obligation is to ensure the writing fully expresses the nature of the study and the logical development of the process you used in conducting the study. Write without personal commentary. You simply report how the study was done. This is the essence of the writing process for this section of your paper.

For a quick review of the elements necessary to the this section of your paper refer to the checklist for the method section in Appendix A on page 131. Use this checklist to ensure that you have included all the expected components for the method section.

7 Preparing the Results

In the results section, when it is required, you report your findings based on the data you have collected. In the method section, you have noted how the data were collected, what instruments were used and what statistical measures or qualitative analyses were used. In the results section, you report on the outcomes of those analyses. The researcher reports in sufficient detail to justify the conclusions of the research. You present or describe only the specific findings you have discovered. You do nothing more. Implications, conclusions, and recommendations are reserved for the discussion section of the study. There are two kinds of research studies that are discussed in this work. One is a quantitative study and the second is a qualitative study. Some researchers may use both in a single study. Each of these kinds of research study requires a different sequence and content for the results section and for the researcher/writer. The sequences for each kind of study are presented below.

Quantitative Results

In quantitative studies you are presenting a study based on a statistical analysis of the data collected. In your method section you identified the population, the variables to be tested, the instruments you used, and the statistical measures used to analyze the data. You will need to briefly review this information for the results

In organizing the results you need to consider the variables being tested and how best to report results in terms of those variables.

section of your study. Once this is done, you present the results. If your study is experimental you are reporting how the intervention or treatment impacted the experimental group compared to the control group who did not use the treatment or the intervention. This can be done through reporting descriptive statistical results, correlational statistical results, or inferential statistical results. You may find that you need to use more than one of these statistical approaches in your analysis of results. Descriptive measures are used to determine mean, median, mode, range, average mean gain, and standard deviation. Inferential statistical measures are used to determine significance. The most common measures used for inferential statistical analyses are the t test and chi square. If you are using a pre test-post test as your instruments to obtain results, questions of reliability and validity may arise. Be sure, whenever necessary, to respond to those questions with the data the readers expect. Correlational statistical analyses are used to show relationships among or between variables. Correlational studies are either predictive or relational and are used to establish a correlational coefficient between or among the variables used. One common correlation measure used for analysis is the Pearson product-moment coefficient or Pearson r. You need to choose the statistical measures pertinent to your study. Some formal studies are based on descriptive statistical analysis, but most researchers use other measures while at times also using descriptive statistics as well. Think through what you are studying and then determine the statistical measures appropriate to that study. In organizing the results you need to consider the variables being tested and how best to report results in terms of those variables. You can report which variable results were more significant than others, but with no personal commentary.

Descriptive statistical analyses are relatively easy to do, but are not as powerful as correlational statistical analyses or inferential statistical analyses. Many graduate students use descriptive statistical measures particularly if the time frame for the study is narrow. If, however, you are going to report significance or lack of significance in your quantitative study you will need to use inferential statistical analyses. If you are reporting how variables correlated with others you use correlational analyses. In both of these statistical analyses you will need to report the level of confidence or significance of the results. These results can be shown through figures or tables included in the narrative. They may also be placed in an appendix. In this section of your work, only the results should be reported. There must be no personal commentary, interpretation, or conclusions about the results. Here you report only on the outcomes and results of your statistical analyses. These are the final results of what you have done and what happened through your study. This section needs to be a cogently and clearly written part of your paper.

Reporting Variables

When you are reporting your findings about individual variables you should identify the variable and then provide the results of your analyses of that variable. This is important to do this because the reader needs to know for which variable or variables you are providing results. Each variable represents, in most cases, data that can be disaggregated according to the demographics of the population involved in the study. Use as much detail as is necessary. The reader will need to know precisely what you have found. The reader needs to know this both in terms of the totality of the data and in terms of data that has been disaggregated for identified groups within the population. You must provide the results accurately and clearly. Sometimes you may want to include figures, graphs, or tables to visually present your results. These can be written as part of the narrative or they can be placed in an appendix. If they are in the appendix, let the reader know by a notation in the narrative.

Surveys, Questionnaires, Interviews

If you have used a survey, questionnaire, or interviews as the measure for data collection, you usually will have a large number of variables you could use for study. These variables emerge from the demographic data in the survey, questionnaire or interviews. You select the variables that are most specific to the purpose of the study. The variables selected should reflect those that are the most important and best illustrate the questions or issues you are investigating. Demographic variables may include age, length of service, assignment, education, gender, and ethnicity. These demographic variables can be used to disaggregate the data in terms of results. When reporting the results from the survey, questionnaire, or interview, write the statement exactly as it appears on the instrument. This statement is then followed by a report of the results in terms of each selected variable using the statistical measures you used to analyze responses to that variable. As the researcher, you may select some of the statements for detailed inclusion in the results. If you do so, you must provide a rationale for your choice of statements and provide a summary of the data from the remaining statements immediately following the analysis of the selected variables. If, in your survey or questionnaire you may have included a space for comments. You need to include pertinent comments in your study. These selected comments are listed immediately following your analysis of the data from the survey or questionnaire and the summary of the statements or questions not analyzed. Sometimes you may wish to have a space for comments after each statement on a survey or a question on a questionnaire. If this is so, the comments can be linked directly to the statement or question. Following your presentation of the results from selected variables, statements, and the summary of the results from the variables, you must prepare a summative statement about the results. This summative statement is designed to bring together the results in a brief way to review the totality of the results and to ensure that the reader has one more opportunity to review the study in terms of the all the results determined through your analyses. This summative statement does not have to be lengthy. If you have determined significance, be sure to report it. Include evidence of variance in terms of demographics and specific variables This summative statement should be brief, but with enough detail to ensure the reader clearly understands your results. You will interpret the meaning of the results in the discussion section of the paper. If you have any questions about how to develop a survey or questionnaire see Appendix F, pages 159–160.

 Qualitative Results

First, the researcher needs to review the process of data collection as noted in the method section and to explain to the reader how the data was collected and analyzed. In qualitative studies you will be dealing with a large amount of data, much of it narrative data, collected through the various observations, interviews and other measures you used. In qualitative studies, you analyze these data. As researcher, you are responsible for the rich thick narrative that tells about both the formative and summative development of the study. Your narrative and findings should be comprehensive, expansive, and richly descriptive. You may need to code or categorize your data as the project develops. These codes or categories can develop and change as the study develops. Be sure to keep a detailed record of what has happened in the study on a daily or regular basis. The information you have gathered in the codes and categories can ensure that the detailed record of your study can be verified. As part of the narrative you may want to use figures or tables. You can do this as part of the narrative. You may also place figures and tables in an appendix. Be sure to follow APA guidelines for figures and tables.

Through the process of analysis you have developed generalizations about the data. Your analyses and results have been gained throughout the qualitative process, but the results will be a synthesis of the generalizations in a descriptive narrative or an emerging theory grounded in the data you have collected. The mode of analysis in qualitative studies is inductive and is done by the researcher. From these generalizations, from the descriptive narrative, and from the emerging theory you have results that can provide meaning and substance for your colleagues. The descriptive narrative must be as complete as possible. Some deem it a richly descriptive narrative (Merriam, 1998). The researcher is narrating the totality of the process involved in your study as well as the emerging information and grounded theory in this narrative. You inform the reader with clarity and a continuity the meaning of the study in terms of results which may include grounded theory.

This is as far as you go in this section of your study. You write clearly, but include all the narrative and all the details necessary. Your narrative establishes the basis for conclusions and recommendations that are made in the discussion section of the paper. For further study you may wish to use descriptive, inferential or correlational statistical analyses with your data. Generalizability and application to similar populations are reserved for the discussion section of the paper.

Writing Tips

Again, when you are writing the results, you are dealing with technical terms as well as mathematical and statistical terms in quantitative studies. In qualitative studies you are dealing with narrative results and emerging theory. You may also be dealing with statistical data and analyses in qualitative studies if they need to be used. You need, however, to make these narrative results clear to the reader. In quantitative studies you must make sure that the reader does not get confused by the narrative, the terms, and the organization of the results. Results of the analysis of each variable should be discussed in simple terms within the narrative as well as in any figures or tables. The numbers need to be presented succinctly and clearly. Avoid simply presenting numbers and statistical data. If you are comparing results in variables make sure you clearly state what you are doing and why you are doing it. As researcher you may need to present the numbers, the data, and the comparisons in a figure or table so they can be seen and more easily understood by the reader. You may include the figures or tables in the text or place them in an appendix. Make sure your explanation of the results is organized and sequenced in a simple and logical order that makes sense to the reader. You may have to work on this explanation to make it readable and cogent for the reader. An introductory paragraph to the results section to inform the reader how you have organized the results including which statements or questions will be specifically analyzed and how you will organize the results section can be very helpful in orienting the reader to a clearer construct of the results section. Results must be understood in order that they could be used by your readers. Write your quantitative results in past or present perfect tense.

In qualitative studies you prepare a narrative of the results. The narrative is written in past tense or present perfect tense. An introductory paragraph on how you organized this section could be included, but may not be necessary. You must make sure that the reader understands how you developed your generalizations and how the theory emerged from the narrative. Great care must be taken in qualitative studies to ensure that the narrative has substance and meaning. You must make sure the findings and results are grounded in the data and that the inferences and emerging theory are logical and provide an evidentiary base. If you use figures or tables as part of your results, be sure to follow APA guidelines. In writing this narrative, the researcher must be sure that no bias, interpretation, or personal perspectives are apparent. Interpretations and personal perspectives are included only in the discussion section of your paper. In writing the results in both quantitative and qualitative studies, be sure that you have written with clarity, with cohesiveness, and in a cogent and careful manner. Use the past or present perfect tense in writing the results section of your study.

For a quick review of the elements necessary for inclusion in the results section refer to the checklist for the results section in Appendix A on page 132. The use of this checklist can help to ensure that you have included all components required for completing the results section of your study.

8

Preparing the Discussion

This is the final narrative section of your paper. It is titled discussion with that word centered one double space below the running head. In this *Handbook* the presentation of the discussion section of the paper is in two parts depending on whether you are writing a review of literature paper or a research study. For a review of literature paper there is a summary of the literature reviewed and presented in the content of the review of literature. For a research study there is a summary of the review of literature, the method section, and the results section in the content of the discussion. Much of the content in both qualitative and quantitative studies is similar, but there are some differences. In both types of studies you follow the summary of the literature reviewed with your interpretation. Finally for both kinds of papers you would draw conclusions and develop recommendations based on the content of the review of literature and your interpretation. In research studies the researcher compares and contrasts the findings of the study with recent and corollary studies in the review of literature and then develop your conclusions and your recommendations. In either type of paper, particularly for shorter papers or studies, you could write this section in narrative form without separating it into its component parts, though you may want to organize it into the component parts of summary, interpretation, conclusions, and recommendations. It is important for you to remember that this is your

> *It is important that you remember that this is your final narrative section of the paper and that it needs, like all the other sections, to be written clearly, carefully, and cogently.*

final narrative section of the paper and that it needs, like all the other sections, to be written clearly, carefully, and cogently.

Review of Literature Paper

In a review of literature paper you do these four things. First, you summarize the literature you have reviewed. Second, you interpret the literature reviewed. Third, you draw conclusions based on your interpretation and the content of the review, and fourth you make recommendations. This is the sequence of the discussion section in the review of literature papers. Be sure to follow this sequence. Do not change the order. Do not bring in any new resources, citations, or additional references in this section of the paper. This is very important. References, citations, and quotations were all included in the review of literature and you do not add to them in the discussion.

Summary

Your first task in the discussion is to summarize the literature you have reviewed for your paper. In a paragraph or a few paragraphs correlated with your categories summarize what you learned from the review of literature. This summary is a recap to help the reader in understanding the interpretation that comes next and to succinctly bring out the salient points of the review of literature. You will need to cite sources so the reader can better understand source of the information. The sources you cite should be your most important sources and should relate to the salient points you want to make in the interpretation. Remember that the sources you cite in the summary are the only ones you use for interpretation. You have cited the most important or salient resources and they are the ones you refer to in the interpretation section of the paper. You use the same sources for the interpretation. Do not add anything more to the summary. You should be non evaluative in your summary. Do not cite new sources in the summary. The summary is written in the past tense or present perfect tense without comment. It is a succinct review of the most important things you found in the review of literature that pertain directly to the purpose of your paper.

Interpretation

This is the part of the discussion section where you process your own interpretation and opinion about the literature you reviewed. Use only the sources noted in the summary. They are the sources you have deemed important and they are the sources you use to interpret the literature. Do not bring in new resources or make provide new citations. In the interpretation you emphasize what you agree with and with what you disagree. You interpret, you compare and contrast, and you bridge the gaps. You give your, ideas, opinions and insights about the literature you reviewed. You interpret the literature. In the interpretation you provide the reader with your own perspective about the literature reviewed. This part of the discussion must be carefully constructed because your interpretations, insights, linkages, and opinions provide the basis for your conclusions and recommendations. The evidence you have brought forward in your review of literature and that you have summarized in this discussion section provide, along with your interpretation, the evidentiary and logical rationale for your conclusions and for your recommendations.

Do not go into great detail. Keep the commentary focused on the literature noted in the summary and your interpretation of that literature. Do not be redundant. Your interpretation must be soundly based on what you have reported in the review of literature. You may write the interpretation in present tense. Think very carefully about what you want to say and how you have thought through the literature so you can write a logical and substantive interpretation that will be clear to the reader and provide the basis for your conclusions and recommendations. You need to ensure that the literature reviewed provided the evidentiary base for your conclusions and recommendations.

Conclusions

The conclusions you have drawn from your review of literature and your interpretation do not need to be lengthy. A sentence like "based on the review of literature and my interpretation of the literature, I have concluded that. . . ." is an appropriate opening sentence. Then you list your conclusions with no elaboration. The conclusions should be written in simple sentences and as briefly and efficiently as possible. You need only enough words to make your conclusion clear. You do not need to go into long or even brief explanations of the conclusions. Those were done in the interpretation section of the discussion. Your conclusions should stand alone as the summative statements about what you have concluded and what the reader should also conclude. The rationale and evidentiary base for your conclusions were made apparent in the interpretation.

Recommendations

Recommendations are statements about what should be done, what should be implemented, or what changes should be made. These recommendations are based solely on your review of literature, your interpretations, and your conclusions. Recommendations, like the conclusions, should not be lengthy or complex. They should draw their evidentiary base from the literature, the interpretation and the conclusions. Recommendations should be written in the same manner as suggested above in the conclusions statement. Almost all papers need recommendations, only a few do not. For review of literature papers this is the final narrative statement of your paper. Do not go into an elaboration, or an explanation. Do not add any new material. State what you recommend as the last narrative statement of your paper. Succinctly stated and carefully written, recommendations can bring a strong closing to your paper.

For a quick review of the elements necessary for the discussion section of review of literature papers refer to the checklist in Appendix A on page 129. The use of this checklist will help ensure that you have included the required elements of the discussion section in your paper.

 ## Research Studies

In the discussion section of a research study whether quantitative or qualitative, you follow the same structure and organization noted for review of literature papers. You summarize, next you interpret, then you draw conclusions, and finally you make recommendations. The organization is the same, but the content varies somewhat. Your obligation in the discussion of research studies is to summarize your findings and how they relate to the study and the literature reviewed. You must ensure that your review of literature provided an evidentiary base for your conclusions and that the review included research studies related to your topic. If you have done this, you are ready to interpret the literature. In the interpretation you discuss the literature and research studies included in your summary. You also note your method, and your results and findings. As you reviewed research studies related to your area of study you can interpret your method and results in terms of those studies. You then draw conclusions and make recommendations on the basis of the literature, the method, and of the results of your study. This chapter or section of your paper is of great importance because you are presenting a professional discussion of what you learned, how you interpreted it, and what you concluded and recommended. This is the final and summative statement of what you have done. You have completed a research study that has importance in your field and you need to disseminate it clearly with emphasis on what the research study means to you and to your colleagues in the profession.

Summary

In this summary component of results you do two things. You summarize the review of literature and you summarize your findings. In the review of literature you focused on the works of researchers, the outcomes of studies, and important sources in your particular area of study. You have prepared the review of literature in terms of the purpose of your study and here you summarize the salient points of that review in terms of the focus and purpose of the study. You then summarize your method and your results in terms of the studies you have reviewed. Your summary of results is a summative statement and should include your most pertinent findings.

Once you have stated your results you need to summarize the literature related to your study. Make sure you have included a summary of studies related to your purpose including their methods and findings. You should focus only the major sources and research studies closely related to your study. You will need to include citations so readers know your major sources. Do not bring in any new sources here, you are simply summarizing your findings and the review of literature. Make sure that what you write in the summary are the salient points within the literature you have reviewed. Remember not to interpret nor elaborate on any findings nor any literature in this section of results. Simply tell what you found and identify and summarize the literature closely related to your study. This summary of the literature reviewed should be used in conjunction with the results from your study. The summary should be written in the past tense and/or present perfect tense.

Interpretation

Here you present your own views on what you have done and what your results mean both in terms of your study and in terms of related literature and other studies in the field. Note how your study related to, correlated with, or was different from other studies in the field. Show where and how your method and the findings of your study agreed with, were similar to, or different from other studies. You compare and contrast, you interpret similarities and differences, and you bridge the gaps. You may include in your narrative figures, tables, and graphs as needed to visually show your results. These would be figures, tables, and graphs already introduced in the results section. From your study do not include new tables, figures or graphs. You can also include figures, tables, and graphs from prior studies specific to your study if they have been included in the review of literature or in the summary. For your interpretation comment only on the sources, tables, figures or graphs you have referred to in the summary. It is only then they can be introduced in this section of the study. These figures, tables, and graphs could also be placed in an appendix.

Discuss any theories or ideas that you have confirmed. Interpret your findings in terms of their consistency with or non consistency with other studies. You compare and contrast your findings with other research in the field and interpret similarities and differences. You must identify significance or lack of significance in terms of the variables tested in quantitative studies if you are using inferential statistical measures. If you are using correlational statistical measures you need to show how identified variables correlate or do not correlate with each other. You must point out in qualitative studies your generalizations and any grounded theory that emerged from the study. You need to emphasize how your results relate to other studies and to the literature you have reviewed in your field of study. The interpretation component of the discussion is extremely important. You write it with care and concern because the successful dissemination of your findings will be based largely on this section of the paper. The generalizability of your results for other similar populations will be based on this interpretation of your study.

As you write the interpretation, readers need to clearly understand what you have found and how your findings relate to the area of study. You emphasize in your closing paragraphs what you feel are the most important findings and the points that highlight what you consider to be important for your colleagues in the field. Be as direct as you need and emphasize the importance of those findings. The final paragraphs of your interpretation should contain the summative statement of your findings, their importance, and how they relate to the area of study. It is from these culminating evidentiary statements in the interpretation that you draw your conclusions and your recommendations.

Conclusions

Your conclusions are drawn directly from the review of literature and the interpretation of the literature, the method, and the results. They should be linked to the summative statements in your interpretation. Conclusions should be written clearly and with the use of only the words needed to state what you have concluded. Conclusions are not lengthy, nor are they convoluted. They are concise and straightforward statements. Conclusions should reflect what you found and carry the conclusive message of your paper. A sentence beginning "based on the review of literature and the findings of this study (paper, thesis, or dissertation), I have concluded that. . . ." This is all that is needed. Do not elaborate or explain. That was done in the interpretation. Both quantitative and qualitative studies follow this pattern. In qualitative studies you should note any grounded theory emerging from your study. State that grounded theory clearly and succinctly as a conclusion. Nothing further needs to be written.

Recommendations

Your recommendations are based on your results, your review of literature, your interpretation, and your conclusions. A recommendation is your statement about what you feel needs yet to be done, on generalizing your findings to specific groups, on implementation and use of what you have concluded, or on further research that should be done in the area of the study. You are making your last narrative statement of the study or paper and your conclusions and recommendations are the final comments you make. Recommendations should be cast in clear, concise, and confident language and attest to a job well done. You do not need to explain the recommendations or elaborate on them. The explanation and narrative about them was done in the interpretation section of the discussion. Recommendations are your final succinct statements of a study. They need to be done with care and attention to the process and to the outcomes. Recommendations are what you project for future studies or for implementation of your results.

For a quick review of the expected elements of the discussion section of a research study refer to the checklist in Appendix A on page 134. The use of this checklist will help ensure that you have included all the required components of this section of your research study.

Writing Tips

These writing tips apply to both review of literature papers and to research studies except where noted. The discussion section of the paper or study can be written as a narrative without second level and third level sections or you can organize the discussion using second and third level heading sections. If your paper or study is relatively brief, do not organize this section into heading sections. If you use second and third level heading sections, you generally name them summary, interpretation, conclusions, and recommendations. Third level headings in a research study could be the names of the categories of your method section such as population, variables, analyses and so forth. If you choose to have second and third level headings you will need to follow APA guidelines. In almost every case, however, you will not use third level heading sections.

In this final section of the paper or study you will continue to use citations to keep the reader informed about the sources to which you are referring. Citations are necessary only in the summary and interpretation components of the discussion. They should not be used for conclusions or recommendations. Do not introduce any new sources in the discussion. Be sure to use the latest APA style and format for all citations. All of your citations should refer to sources within the review of literature. For the interpretation section remember that you use only the information and sources provided in the summary. In the interpretation section you point out what was most important in the literature as it relates to your interpretation.

In a research study you also need to identify your findings and interpret them as they relate to the literature you reviewed. In both quantitative and qualitative studies you express your own opinion only in the interpretation category of the discussion section. Express your personal opinions along with your conclusions and recommendations. This chapter or section is the only place in the paper or study where you present personal opinions and interpretations. This is where you can be emphatic and confident. This is where you make the final determination about the importance and worth of your paper or your study. Make sure that the final paragraphs in the interpretation clearly state what you consider to be most important to the reader. This becomes the link to your conclusions and your recommendations.

While some of the writing in this section is in the past tense or present perfect tense, in particular the summary, you can present your interpretations, opinions, conclusions, and recommendations in the present tense. Your recommendations can, in some instances, be in the future tense. In the discussion you present your summary and findings. You also tell the reader how you interpreted the literature and the findings. In terms of your findings you both interpret them and suggest meanings. Be sure that the meaning of the study is consistent with the results. In the interpretation you will also need to compare and contrast your findings with related studies you reviewed. The review of literature should provide an integral part of the evidentiary base for your study. This is also where you present your opinions. In the discussion you compare and contrast, bridge the gaps, judge and interpret. Here is where you conclude and where you recommend. Indeed, this is what the discussion is all about.

In the interpretation component of the discussion you can use the personal pronoun I or if there is more than one author the personal pronoun we. It is wise, however, to minimize the use of I or we. Let what has been written speak for itself. Do not, however, refer to yourself as the author. You can also write in the present tense except in the summary. When you make recommendations you may, if appropriate, use the future tense. You have the opportunity, in this section, to reflect you personal perspectives and opinions. You will strongly support your professional findings and positions in terms of the interpretation, conclusions, and recommendations as long as they are supported by evidence from the review of literature and from the results. This is where you react to the issues, problems, and questions inherent within the paper. You do this based on the review of literature and the findings if you did a research paper. You do not bring in any new resources. What you have done needs to rest on its own integrity. You present your paper from your own professional perspective.

When you have completed this section of the paper you have finished a well organized and properly sequenced professional paper. Be sure to edit the rough drafts and refine your paper until you are satisfied that it is the best that you can do. One good way to do this is to read it aloud. You can quickly hear problems of organization, continuity, and syntax, and make the necessary corrections. Another good way to edit the paper is to have a peer or someone else critique it. Be sure to find someone who will be objective and provide positive suggestions and ideas for you in terms of editing your paper. Once the final editing is done, you will have completed the professional preparation of your paper. It will be ready for a professional reader to review it and ready for publication.

In writing your paper, do not procrastinate. Start as soon as you have defined the topic. Define the topic as quickly as possible. You know that you have a deadline to meet, so follow a schedule. Sometimes the schedule may be set by the instructor. Sometimes you need to develop a personal timeline for completion of the paper or study. Above all, do not wait until late in the class time frame or the report schedule to start your paper. In some instances the instructor or supervisor may be willing to review your paper or consult with you if you have any problems. Take advantage of those reviews and consultations. If your instructor or supervisor will review the paper, turn in a rough draft or what you have completed at the time designated by the instructor or supervisor. The review by the instructor or supervisor as well as consultations with others can help you produce a much better paper, perhaps one that will be published in some context.

Just a word about plagiarism. Remember that you can use direct quotes, you can paraphrase, and you summarize a writer's work. You must, however, always cite the source. Using an author's words directly without citation constitutes plagiarism and will result in a seriously marred paper or a failing grade. Your reader will check for plagiarism. Start gathering resources in an organized manner. Note all the bibliographical information for any source reviewed and cited in your paper. Annotate pertinent resources. Also write down appropriate quotes and key them to page numbers or heading sections. Cite them in your paper. Once you have identified the categories, put your sources along with quotes and bibliographical information in categories or on colored cards so they are keyed to your categories. Develop a personal system for organizing and categorizing information. Sometimes different colored cards can help you organize material. In writing your paper, set a time line and keep to it. Build into the time line checkpoints and benchmarks for completing certain sections and for editing purposes. Formal papers take consistent and careful effort and time. Be sure that you put in as much time as you will need. Keep this *Handbook* close by for reference and as a resource for writing your paper. Best wishes to you in your writing process and congratulations on finishing this last narrative section of your paper. For a quick review of the discussion section see checklists pages 133 and 134.

9 Preparing the References

The final section of your paper or study is the reference section. This section is titled references. It is not a part of the narrative, but it is an integral and essential section of your paper and is numbered as part of the paper with the short version of running head all in caps. In this section you include only the references you have cited in the paper. Do not include any other references. This is not a bibliography. It is a list of sources you have referred to in your paper. Be sure that every entry and every line in the reference section is double-spaced. Your reader will check the citations and references carefully and match them with each other. Your reader will also check to ensure that you have followed the format of the APA. It is, therefore, essential that you follow the APA format. You will find clear and specific formats for all kinds of references in the sixth edition of the *Publication Manual of the American Psychological Association*. A list of the most common references is also provided for you in the Appendix E beginning on page 155 of this handbook. It should be noted here that personal communications are not included in the reference section. See page 154 for a discussion of how to format them. Personal communications are included only in the narrative sections of the paper, not in the reference section. You must ensure that all references are alphabetized by author. If no author is listed for the source, the title of the source is used. If there is no title a concise descriptor of the source is used. Again, all references are listed

> In this section you include only the references you have cited in the paper. Do not include any other references. This is not a bibliography.

in alphabetic sequence including those without an author named. The reference format is called a hanging reference. This means that the first line of each reference is justified to the left margin. Succeeding lines in the reference are tabbed with the same number of spaces you used for the tabbing of your paper. If you are referencing an internet source, include the pathway and be sure the pathway is not underlined and that it is always written in black with an APA approved typeface. Do not put a period after the pathway unless it is a part of it. In the latest edtion of the *Publication Manual* you do not include the date you downloaded or reviewed the internet source. The sample references for your paper or study are found on pages 155–157. This is only a partial list; check the latest edition *Publication Manual* for a more complete presentation of references. These sample references are examples of how your reference section should be organized and formatted.

In the latest edition of the *Publication Manual,* the APA has initiated a Digital Object Identifier (DOI) system for articles published that have online links. "A DOI is a unique alphanumeric string assigned by a registration agency (Internatinal DOI Foundation) to identify content and to provide a persistent link to its location on the Internet" (*Publication Manual,* 2010, p. 189). A DOI number always begins with the number 10 and contains a prefix and suffix separated by a slash. See the sample reference on page 155 for how to use the DOI in the references. It should be noted that many Internet resources do not include a DOI number.

For a quick review of the elements of the reference section, please refer to the checklist for preparation of references found in Appendix A on page 135. The use of this checklist will help ensure that you have completed the required components of the reference section.

Writing Tips

It should be noted that you must follow the format and sequence of elements of the each of the kinds of references you use. Indeed, your references should be exact in terms of the sequence of elements. Please refer to Appendix E on pages 155–157 for samples of the most common references. Check the *Publication Manual* for additional reference samples.

Chapter

10 Bibliography and Appendixes

It should be noted here that you may include a bibliography and appendixes in your paper. A bibliography and appendixes are not essential elements of the paper, but you may want to include them if your instructor, or your supervisor feel they are needed. A bibliography is a list of resources not in the references, but which pertain to the topic or the study. Do not include sources that do not correlate with your topic or to your study. The bibliography is not a part of your narrative paper, nor is it a part of the reference section. If you include a bibliography as additional source material, it is a good idea to do a brief annotation of each resource so the reader can select material of interest that will provide for supplemental personal reading in the field. The annotation is blocked and begins one double space below the entry. It is not indented. It should be brief and focused. It should contain material that could supplement a reader's study of the material corollary and ancillary to your paper or study. The bibliography immediately follows the reference section of your paper. A bibliography has a running head for each page and follows the number sequence of the paper or the study.

Appendixes, if you have included them, are placed following the reference section of your paper and the bibliography if one is included. Center the word "Appendix " as a level one heading one double space below the running head. Be sure it is in bold. When there is more than one appendix, they are usually lettered A, B, C, D and so forth. If the paper has only one appendix, it is simply referred to as

> A bibliography is a list of resources not in the references, but which pertain to the topic or the study.

the appendix. Each appendix must have a title. Appendices are listed as such in the table of contents if one or more are included in your paper or study. Appendixes may include tables, figures, statistical information, illustrations or narrative, and any additional supplemental material you feel is important for reader information. In the body of the paper, usually in the method, the results, or in the discussion sections, you can refer to the appendix pertinent to the information or to the interpretation presented. Be sure to follow APA style and format for all appendices.

Writing Tips

For a quick review of the elements of the bibliography see the checklist for bibliography in Appendix A page 138. For a review of the elements of appendices refer to the checklist for appendixes in Appendix A page 137. The use of these checklists will help ensure that you have completed the required components of the bibliography and the appendix in the correct format.

11 Common Problems in Writing Formal Papers

Over the years we have read thousands of formal papers. We are, in this section, focusing on some of the more common errors, problems, and issues we have found in student writing. The *Publication Manual of the American Psychological Association* provides an excellent source for helping you in the writing process. The information in this *Handbook* is consistent with that manual. There are other fine manuals and resources available to you as well, some of which we have already cited. What we have done here, however, is to provide a compendium of common problems, issues, and errors in graduate and formal papers we have read over the past years. They are listed in alphabetic order. We consistently find these problems, issues, and errors in papers and studies. Be cognizant of them as you write your own paper or your research study.

Abstract

The abstract is noted as page two of your paper. It consists of from 150 to 250 words and includes the purpose of the paper or study and salient points you have found. Major findings, if you have written a research study, are included. Major conclusions and recommendations should also be included. The abstract is not indented, nor is it centered. It is blocked and justified on the left margin. The abstract is double-spaced. Avoid personal pronouns and information about sources.

> An ellipsis is used when you leave a word or words out of a direct quote for clarity of meaning.

Agreement

Referents should agree in gender and number. This statement encapsulates the nature of these kinds of errors. Verbs and pronouns should agree in gender and number with the subject. In this era of politically correct writing, we have frequently read papers where the author has used a single subject such as student and has then used they, their, or them rather than having noun pronoun agreement. This is not acceptable in formal papers. You can use he/she if you wish, but avoid this as much as possible. In most instances you can, through careful writing, avoid the heeshees and remain consistent in terms of subject pronoun agreement. There should also be agreement in gender and number with subject and verb. Review your paper carefully to correct any such errors.

Among and Between

You should note that when you are comparing and contrasting or making a statement discussing difference between pairs and groups you use *among* when referring to more than two or more than groups of two. You use *between* when referring only to groups of two or to pairs of groups.

Anthropomorphisms

An anthropomorphism occurs when ascribing human characteristics to animals or inanimate objects. Remember that research cannot say, infer, demonstrate, show, or indicate. Only researchers, writers, or authors can write, infer, demonstrate, show, or indicate. This is a very common error by writers of formal papers including some that occur in published papers and books. In fact, it is the most common error in papers we have read. Avoid anthropomorphisms. They indicate sloppiness of style, careless construction, and poor writing.

Author Reference

Use the personal pronoun I with great care throughout the paper. Do not use the third person or refer to yourself as the author of the paper or study. Whenever you need to refer to yourself, use the personal pronoun "I." If the paper has two or more authors use "we." Minimize the use of "I" throughout the paper. Use it when you note why I chose the paper in the introduction and when you interpret, conclude, and recommend in the discussion section. Even in those instances, use personal pronouns with discretion. It is seldom, if ever, used in other sections of the paper.

Brackets

Brackets are used to insert material in a quotation, usually by the author of the paper or study. Brackets can be used to clarify a point, or to provide for continuity and sequence in the quotation. Brackets can also be used to point out an error in grammar or syntax.in a quote. A word or words are used in brackets. The term [sic] in a bracket indicates a spelling error.

Capitalization

Only proper nouns are capitalized. Names of content areas such as mathematics, science, and language arts are not capitalized. Only English in content areas is capitalized. The terms "special education" and "English language learners" are written as shown.

Categories

Classes or divisions in a scheme of organization. For formal writing purposes, the term "categories" has been replaced. See "headings."

Citations

Citations are simple to do, but if in doubt refer to the APA *Manual*. The usual citation is the author's last name followed by a comma and the year of publication. If no date of publication is given use the initials n.d. in lower case. This information is in parentheses. You may use the author's name as part of a sentence. If you do, follow it with the year of publication in parentheses. When a work has no author use the first two or three words of the title. If there is no author or title use a brief descriptor of the content not to exceed two words. These are the first two or three words of your reference. If you are using a direct quote, you must use the author's name, the year, and the page number of the quotation. Direct quotes for a book with no author listed are in italics (*Publication Manual*). Direct quotes of less than forty words require quotation marks. Direct quotes of forty or more words are blocked without the use of quotation marks. If the quote is from a short internet article use the abbreviation "para." followed by the paragraph number. You may also use the paragraph symbol. Check the most recent edition of the APA *Publication Manual* for additional information on electronic citations and references.

Colloquialisms

Avoid the use of colloquial language or slang. In a formal paper, this is unacceptable except in rare circumstances or unless the colloquialism occurs in a direct quote. A colloquialism is informal or idiomatic speech or writing and should not be used in formal papers. The most common colloquialism we have seen in papers is "a lot" meaning many or frequent. Writers forget that a lot is a small area of ground on which structures can be built. Avoid also the use of idioms, regionalisms, and slang expressions.

Ellipses

An ellipsis is used when you leave a word or words out of a direct quote. It is used for clarity of meaning. An ellipsis is shown by three dots to signify that a word or words have been omitted from the quote. You make an ellipsis by doing a dot with a space between dots three times to show words omitted. Use four dots with a space between each dot when the omitted words occur in two or more sentences. Generally do not begin or end a quote with ellipses.

Headings

There are five levels of headings accepted by the APA. Most papers use only the first three. Level one headings also called title case headings are used for titles of major sections or chapters of the paper. They are centered one double space below the running head. They are in upper case and lower case with only articles in lower case. They are in bold with the exception of the title page, the abstract, and references. Level two headings are titles of sections of the paper. They are justified on the left margin and are on a separate line from preceding and succeeding text. They are in bold and are capitalized except for articles. Level three headings are what were called subcategories in previous versions of APA. They are indented one tab space. They are in boldface and only the first word and proper nouns are capitalized. They end with a period and the text begins one space after the period. Level four and level five headings are seldom used in papers or studies. They may be used for dissertations and more extensive studies.

Hyphens

A punctuation mark (-) used to divide or to compound words, word elements, or numbers. Do not end a line or begin a line of the narrative with a hyphen. Use hyphens as defined by the APA. Self, when it is linked to a characteristic is always hyphenated. Non does not need a hyphen. It can stand alone or be linked to its characteristic such as *nondirective.*

If as Conditional

When writing in the past tense always use the word *were* when following the noun or pronoun with a plural past tense form of to be. When using the word if, it is followed by the word *were*. If, in this sense, is a conditional and requires the use of were.

Justification

The paper or study is justified only on the left margin. Do not justify on the right margin of the paper. All lines of citations of forty or more words are justified one tab space from the left margin. The right margin is not justified in the paper or study except for page numbers after the running head. The numbers of the pages in the table of contents and throughout the paper or study are justified on the right margin. Quotations of more than forty words are blocked and justified one tab space from the left margin in all lines. Quotation marks are not used to open or close a blocked quote. If a quotation is included in a blocked quote use only one quotation mark single quotation marks or apostrophe at the beginning and end of the quote within the blocked quote.

Language

Use specific and precise language. Eliminate redundancies. Do not use slang expressions or colloquialisms. Check your choice of words and make sure that you are saying what you want to say with an economy of expression. Say only what needs to be said. Avoid jargon or the continual use of technical language. While some technical or professional terminology may be necessary, the continual use of such language can be distracting and irritating to the reader. Presentation of ideas must be orderly and sequential. Use punctuation to provide for clarity and continuity. Use transitional words and pronouns to provide for additional clarity and continuity. Use simple sentences most of the time. Use compound or complex sentences only when necessary.

Numbers

Numbers zero through nine must be written out. Numbers ten and over can be written in their Arabic form. Numbers are always written out at the beginning of a sentences such as: Seventy-four percent.

Quotations

There is an expectation that you use direct quotes in your paper. If the quote is less than 40 words, it is included in the narrative with quotation marks at the beginning of the quote and at the end of the quote. All quotations must have a citation with a page number or a paragraph number. For quotations of 40 or more words, each line of the quotation is blocked one tab space from the left margin. If there is a quotation within the quotation use a single quotation mark (') at the beginning and end of the quote within the quotation.

Personal Communications

These refer to discussions with people consulted or interviewed during the preparation of your paper. Personal communications can also be memos, e-mails, and other electronic resources. You may quote or paraphrase the information you have gained from them in the narrative sections of your paper. Most frequently these occur in the review of literature. If the personal communication is used for a direct quote follow the format for quotations. Use initials and surname in the citation. Personal communications are cited as follows: J. Doe, (personal communication, June 21, 2010) or (J. Doe, personal communication, June 21, 2010) They are cited in the text only and are not included in the reference section.

Plagiarism

Plagiarism means to copy someone's work and claim it or infer it to be your own. You must provide a citation for every statement in your paper except the selection of the topic and why you chose the topic, in the interpretion component of the discussion, and in the conclusions, and recommendations. For every other part of the paper or study you must give credit to the source. Your reader will check for plagiarism. If you have plagiarized content in any part of your paper it will result in a failing grade or a rejection of your paper.

Redundancy

While redundancy may sometimes be used in the discussion section to be emphatic, it should be studiously avoided throughout your paper. Your paper is stronger without it. Do not be emphatic through redundancy. If you wish to emphasize a point in the discussion section, let the reader know that you feel it is important. It may sometimes be necessary to restate an idea, thought, or interpretation for clarity and emphasis, but do it in language different than the original so that it becomes a logical followup to what you have already written.

Referents

Be very careful about referents. Be sure the reader clearly understands what you are referring to when you use a pronoun to refer to the subject. Referent problems occur most often when you are citing an author and continue discussing the work. Include a restatement of the author's name or the subject of the discussion no later than three to six sentences from the last referent. Referents should agree in gender and number. Do not use we or our to refer to groups of people in your profession. Always use the name of the group of people to whom you are referring.

Spacing

Just a simple reminder. Everything in your paper is double-spaced. The use of any other spacing constitutes a format error. The reference section and direct quotes of more than 40 words are double spaced along with every other section of your paper. Text begins one double space below the page header. Improper spacing, as has been noted, is a format error. Single spacing may be used in tables and graphs when necessary. Single spacing can also be used, when necessary, in appendixes.

Subcategories

Sub divisions within a category or section. For formal writing purposes, this term has been eliminated in the sixth edition of the *Manual*. See "headings" for new organization of sections. It corresponds to third level headings.

Superscript and Subscript

Do not use superscript or subscript except in mathematical or scientific formulae or as approved by the APA. Do not use superscript in the reference section when referring to the edition of a book.

Syntax

Sentence structure is important. Write clearly, sequentially, and logically. Use simple sentences for the most part. Say only what needs to be said. Compound and complex sentences should be used only when needed and to clarify the information presented. Comma splices (sometimes called comma faults), run on sentences, and fragments are major syntax errors and could seriously affect the quality of your paper and your grade. Major syntax errors would certainly be noted by an editor or publisher. Fragments occur most frequently when you begin a sentence with an adverb. Be sure to review your paper for syntax errors.

Tense

This is one of the most common errors we have seen in papers. In formal papers you use the past tense or the present perfect tense consistently in the abstract, introduction, and review of literature. You also use the past or present perfect tense in the method and results sections of a research study. The present perfect tense refers to an action that did not occur at a specific defined time or occurred in the past and is continuing. Remember that when the reader reviews your paper you have already completed the paper. All literature or research you cite in your paper has been completed. The only exception for the use of the past or present perfect tense is within direct quotes when the writer you are quoting uses a tense other than the past tense or present perfect tense. In the discussion section of your paper you use the past tense or present perfect tense in the summary or when referring to the literature reviewed. You may use the present tense, the future tense, or other tenses in the discussion section of your paper or study when you are interpreting, comparing and contrasting, expressing your professional opinions, drawing conclusions or making recommendations.

That and Who

Use who or whom to refer to humans. Use that or which to refer to animals. This is a frequent error and needs to be avoided.

Typeface

"The use of a uniform typeface and font size enhances readability for the editor [or reader]. . . . The preferred typeface for APA publications is Times New Roman, with 12 point font size" (*Publication Manual*, 2010, p. 228). No superscript or subscript may be used except in specified scientific or mathematics symbols or formulae. Do not use superscript in the reference section. Eliminate any color other than black in the reference section including internet pathways.

Voice

Use the active voice rather than the passive voice in your writing in most instances. The active voice is a direct communicator of ideas and meaning and the active voice fits well into the context of formal papers. The passive voice is used only when you want to focus on the object of the action or the recipient of the action. Proper use of voice makes for clearer communication of the content of your paper.

12 Formal Writing Conventions

Formal writing is a style used by those who are preparing papers, reviews of literature, research studies, and formal documents for a specific audience. As noted in the preface, formal writing is a pristine exercise in clarity, continuity, and cogent thinking. Following the conventions of formal writing helps ensure that this occurs in papers, documents, and research studies. Formal writing is consistently used when writing a review of literature paper or a research study. Formal writing is used for some reports, for monographs, and for a variety of other formal documents. Formal writing can also be used for preparing narrative journal articles or formal reports to designated groups. Formal writing is a style that can be easily learned. It does, however, have certain conventions which need to be followed and used in the preparation of the document you plan to submit. Listed below are some of the conventions of formal writing.

Organization

Formal writing is organized into sections or chapters according to the length of the paper. Generally in papers under fifty pages one does not use chapters. Use section headings. For longer papers, monographs, or narrative documents chapters may be used as headings with the title of the chapter centered one double space below the number of the chapter that is written in upper case Roman numerals. When writing

> *Formal writing is a pristine exercise in clarity, continuity, and cogent thinking.*

a review of literature paper, three sections will be used. They are introduction, review of literature, and discussion. The full title of the paper is used in the introduction. The next sections are entitled review of literature and discussion. For research studies there are five sections. They are introduction, review of literature, method, results, and discussion. The full title is used in the introduction. The succeeding sections are entitled as review of literature, method, results, and discussion. For theses or dissertations of more than fifty pages, these five sections are sometimes noted as chapters. Sections are not called chapters in APA, but check with your instructor or your supervisor if you are writing a thesis, dissertation, or major paper to see if chapter terminology is expected. Turabian (2007) suggests the term chapter in place of the APA designation of sections. In writing formal papers for journals, sections may not be necessary. For formal reports and documents, follow a narrative sequence or any structure set by the organization to which the document or formal report is to be submitted. This may entail identifying sections by specific names needed for the audience. An abstract of from 150-250 words follows the title page and precedes content. A table of contents may be expected, particularly in research studies, monographs, and in some formal reports or documents. Tables of content are numbered in lower case Roman numerals. Table of contents numbers are justified on the right margin.

 **Syntax**

Formal writing should be straightforward, strong and cogent. Formal writing should be easily understood by the readers. You are generally writing for audiences familiar with the area of the study or for audiences who want to learn more about the topic or study. Syntax is very important. Most of the time use short simple sentences. Use complex or compound sentences only when necessary. Usually over eighty percent of the sentences should be simple sentences. Use technical language only when needed. The well wrought paper will flow effectively if sentences are clearly understood by the reader. Avoid syntactical usage that would result in choppiness and reduce the cogency of the paper. This sometimes happens if only simple sentences are over used. Compound and complex sentences can be used occasionally to make the flow of the paper smoother and more efficient. Do not add extra wording to sentences or try to impress the reader with your erudition. Use the active voice in almost all formal writing. Remember that verbosity is the last refuge of mediocrity. Say only what needs to be said and say it mostly in short, clear, and carefully wrought simple sentences. The appropriate use of syntax can greatly enhance your paper.

Related to syntax is the structure of paragraphs. Paragraphs should not be lengthy. Four to fifteen lines should encompass the length of a paragraph. In certain instances they may be longer, but those instances are rare. Paragraphs are organized around a specific topic. Often the topic is stated in the initial sentence, but it can be noted later in the paragraph. The meaning of the paragraph may, however, become apparent only through the whole narrative of the paragraph. The effective use of paragraphs can strengthen the paper and provide for fluent structure, clarity, and sequence for readers.

Word Usage

The selection of the right word is very important in formal writing. Use the precise word in each sentence for clarity of meaning. Word usage in an appropriate syntactical structure can ensure continuity and cogency. Keep a dictionary and a thesaurus close by for reference when writing a formal paper. The right words in the right place are strong virtues in formal writing. It is necessary that you avoid colloquialisms, idiomatic expressions, and slang. You are writing a formal paper and the use of those kinds of words or phrases can deter from meaning, bring about an uncomfortable response from the reader, and can reduce the the sequence and flow of the paper. Avoid the use of too many descriptors for nouns. When several descriptors are used, break them out into individual sentences.

It is also very important to avoid value oriented words throughout the paper with the exception of portions of the discussion when interpreting, drawing conclusions, or making recommendations. Even in those portions of the discussion they should be used sparingly, if at all. The use of value oriented words earlier can, and usually do, show your biases and your opinions. These have no place in a formal paper except in the interpretation, conclusions, and recommendations. You are not writing a polemic. You are writing a formal paper that should be as objective as possible until you interpret, analyze, conclude, and recommend. These interpretations, analyses, conclusions, and recommendations are based on your objective review of literature and on the methods and results you have found if you are writing a research study. As you review your paper, look also for words that are not precise or which can be interpreted in more than one way. Change, whenever possible, any word that could be interpreted in more than one way. Make changes for precision of language and for the continuity and cogency of the paper. The proper use of words is essential in any formal paper.

In writing your paper or study also avoid the use of words that have multiple meanings or can be interpreted in a number of ways. We call these "fuzzy" words. They deter from the clarity and continuity of your papers. It is always important to choose the right word and to use those words for building a strong sequential, clear, and cogent paper or study.

Tense

The tenses of choice in formal writing are past and present perfect. The past tense is used consistently throughout the paper for citations and references to the sources you have used. The past tense or present perfect tense are used in every section of the paper with the exception that you may use the present tense or the future tense in the interpretation, conclusion, and recommendation components of the discussion section. The only other exception occurs when a direct quote is used in the paper and contains a tense other than past or present perfect. Present perfect tense is used for an event or issue that started in the past and has been continuing. In the body of the paper the use of past or present perfect is consistent until the discussion section of the paper. In the discussion section the present tense can be used, as noted above, for the interpretation, the conclusions, and the recommendations. When writing the recommendations the future tense may be used.

The rationale for using the past tense or present perfect tense is that every source cited or reference has already been written. Even citations from the internet have been posted before you read the paper. A further rationale is that your readers will have read your paper as something that was done in the past and that they are reading from that perspective. This may be one of the conventions that may be the most difficult to accommodate because writers are conditioned to write in the present tense or other tenses. It is important, however that you adhere strictly to this convention when writing formal papers.

Quotations and Paraphrases

Every statement of information in a formal paper with a few exceptions must be based upon the ideas and writings of the authors of your sources. The exceptions in the body of the paper are in the purpose statement and the rationale for selecting topic. Additional exceptions are in the interpretation, conclusions, and recommendations. No opinions, personal perspectives, or added comment can be made in any other section of a formal paper. Every new fact, idea, information, or point of view must come from an identified source and be cited. Direct quotes from the source may be used. Paraphrases may also be used. They must be cited. Each quotation or paragraph must have a citation. Direct quotes of less than forty words are shown by quotation marks at the beginning of the quotation and at the end of the quotation. This is followed by the author, the date, and the page number from the source. Quotations of forty or more words are blocked and are not opened and closed with quotation marks, A quotation within a blocked quote is opened and closed with a single quotation mark or apostrophe ('). Blocked quotes are followed by a citation of the author, year of publication, and page number.

You may use paraphrases from a source. These paraphrases must be documented by a citation. Paraphrases are used when you summarizing an author's ideas, narrative, or perspective. Do not add any personal comments or reaction to the paraphrase. You do that in the interpretation component of the discussion section. Your reader will almost always check your sources and will be aware of any personal comments you may have added. It is very important to remember this when writing a formal paper.

References and Bibliography

References and bibliographies are two different elements of a formal paper. References are a compilation of the sources you have cited in the paper. They are listed alphabetically by last name of author. Use only initials for first and middle name. A reference section is required for formal papers in which citations have been made. You need to follow the style manual your university, organization, or corporation recommends. We are using the format provided by the American Psychological Association in their latest publication manual in this *Handbook.* Be sure that you follow the structure of the format for each reference. There are more than a hundred variations and you must select the one that needs to be used for every specific reference. When making citations and preparing for their inclusion in the reference section of the paper, be sure you have all the correct bibliographical information. Many readers will refer to the reference section when citations are made in the body of the work.

Bibliographies are not necessarily a part of a formal paper. They can, however be included as a separate section following the reference section. A bibliography is an alphabetized list of sources pertinent to the area of study, but not included in the reference section. Do not include any of the sources listed in the reference section of the paper or study. Make sure that the sources listed in the bibliography pertain to the topic of the paper. To ensure that the reader understands this, a brief annotation for each work in the bibliography can be included. We recommend a brief annotation for each listing in the bibliography. Annotations can be brief, but must reflect a relationship to the topic and/or to a particular heading level section. Bibliographies without annotations can be included, but are of little use for the reader. The purpose of the bibliography is to provide the reader with additional sources directly related to the topic for further reading and study. We, therefore, strongly recommend an annotated bibliography if one is included in your paper or study.

Other Formal Writing Conventions

There are a number of other conventions. Among these are the elimination of anthropomorphisms, the use of the active voice, avoiding redundancies, appropriate use of ellipses, the use of the correct typefaces and font size, the proper use of that and who, among and between, and references to the author. All these and others are discussed in the *Handbook.* They are discussed in the section on Common Problems in Writing Formal papers. Please refer to that section of the *Handbook* that pertains to any questions about these and other formal writing conventions. In the *Handbook* you will not only find information about the writing conventions mentioned above, but useful tips on organization, writing, sequence, and structure. Explanations of many of these conventions are found in the Common Problems in Writing Formal Papers section of the

Handbook. Please also refer to the grammar section for additional guidelines and assistance in writing. The grammar section of this *Handbook* can also be of help to you. Be sure to check the index for specific help. Information is keyed to the page or pages of the *Handbook and* where it can be found through the index.

 ## Additional Applications

Formal writing conventions are used in many other contexts. If you are in education and are working on policy or are on a committee working on curriculum, instruction, evaluation, policy, or any other issue, formal writing conventions need to be used for any papers to be presented or reports to be prepared. Narrative reports of action research done within the classroom or the school also need to be written using formal writing conventions. In education, business or other professions, formal writing conventions must be used for white papers, reports, committee summaries, monographs, theses, dissertations, personal response papers, writing online and other formal instruments. The use of formal writing conventions can be applied in any context where there is a need for a clear, concise, and well-wrought document. In any of these contexts the use of formal writing conventions can be a responsive and lucid organizational structure available to meet the needs of the writers and for their presentations. We encourage the use of these conventions in any professional exercise involving, study, analysis, synthesis, and evaluation. Formal writing conventions can meet the needs of people in any profession and in any circumstance where reporting is needed.

 ## Summary

What we have done in this section of the *Handbook* is to cluster together some of the major conventions of formal writing as well as to briefly refer to others. In some cases this is redundant to what was presented earlier in the *Handbook*. We felt, however, that this reiteration was necessary and positive and would provide a quick overview of formal writing conventions as well as an additional perspective on protocols that must be followed in formal papers. This focus on formal writing conventions provides yet another perspective on developing your formal paper, report, or document. We have provided a brief insight into a number of the conventions of formal writing. It can serve as a strong and useful adjunct to the *Handbook*. Our best wishes to you as you work on and complete your formal papers utilizing the *Handbook* and this summary of formal writing conventions.

Writing Tips

For a quick review of these conventions, refer to the checklist on conventions of formal writing found in Appendix A page 136. The use of the checklist will provide a further review of your paper in terms of formal writing.

Preparing Formal Reports or White Papers

Chapter

13

In preparing formal reports, also called white papers, the conventions of formal writing are followed consistently. Formal reports or white papers are specific to identified audiences. It is imperative that any parameters or expectations concerning the audience for which you are writing are specifically followed. Your purpose in a formal report is to explore an issue or problem, examine the elements within the problem, review literature pertinent to the problem or issue, discuss them, and develop conclusions and recommendations that could provide information about the problem or issue and which could resolve or ameliorate the problem or issue. The formal report or white paper has four parts. They are introduction, background, current practices, and conclusions and recommendations. Your report will also include citations of literature reviewed, any personal communications, and references.

Introduction

In the introduction you will first state the purpose of the report or white paper clearly and concisely. You will also establish the importance of the report or white paper by providing general information about the topic, problem, or issue. In the importance of the report or white paper you will need to cite sources from literature

> *The formal report or white paper has four parts. They are introduction, background, current practices, and conclusions and recommendations.*

pertinent to the problem. Sources could be from print material or online material. You may also use personal communications with those involved in the issue and cite those personal communications. Personal communications are listed in the narrative of the paper, but not in the reference section. Through these citations and personal communications, you establish the importance of the report. Further, you need to provide a brief review of the existing situation. Your introduction should be relatively short and should inform your audience clearly and concisely your purpose, your definition of the problem or issue, and why the report or white paper is important to the audience. Through identifying the importance of the report or white paper, you establish the need for the report or white paper.

You further show why it is important to the audience. After you have defined the problem you will present information on the existing situation and the current status of the issue or problem. In the introduction all these pertinent factors and the current status of the problem or issue are succinctly presented, resources are cited to establish both the need for the report or white paper and to clearly and succinctly define the issue or problem presented from information and interviews with people involved in the problem as well as literature about similar issues and problem. Through the introduction, the stage is set for the next section of the white paper or formal report. That section is the background.

Background

In the background section of your formal report or white paper you provide information specific to your company, your community, your school, or your school district. You review how the issue or problem has been being addressed by personnel assigned to it and to those responsible for oversight. You review current processes, practices, and interventions already in place in the context of the problem being reviewed. Further, you review the history of the problem. You explore how the problem or the issue has been addressed earlier and what changes have taken place since the problem was initially found to be an issue. You note changes and development in terms of the history of the issue. You will also show how it is affecting or impacting personnel, residents, teachers, parents, students, management, and administrators. It is your obligation in formal reports or white papers to include all this background information as well as the history of the problem.

You will, in addition, include information on how other companies, corporations, government entities, schools, or school districts have dealt with the issue or similar problems. To gather this information you may need to interact with participants, review historical documents, conduct interviews, and cite related literature. Material in the background section should focus only the problem or issue you are reviewing and discussing. It should not be too broad in its scope. Include citations and personal communications as part of the background information. In this section of your formal report or white paper it is essential for the audience to gain a perspective on how you have defined the issues and problems in context and how they have been addressed historically. The audience should also be informed about how the issue or problem and the history of how this problem or issue has been handled by other similar companies, schools, or school districts. It is important that this section of your paper be clearly, concisely, and cogently written. All conventions of formal writing must be followed in this section of the white paper.

Current Practices/Opinions

Here you build on what you have presented in the background section. You have already defined the issues or the problems, you have put them in historical contexts, and explained existing perspectives and approaches. You have also discussed how similar companies, schools, or districts have been dealing with the same kinds of issues or problems. In this section you go into further detail about the current status of the issue or problem in your corporation, company, school, or district. You also provide an overview of current practices by institutions facing the same or similar problems or issues. In your formal paper or white paper you will review optional approaches, perspectives, ideas, and opinions. This is a key element for this section of your formal report or white paper. You need to present these optional approaches, perspectives, and opinions logically and, if possible, in hierarchical order. You need to explain them thoroughly and very specifically so that your audience will clearly understand each of them, be able to react to them, to think about them, and to ponder them. Intrinsically in this section you are also presenting evidence for your conclusions and recommendations. You need investigate the issue thoroughly in terms of how it has been addressed up to this point.

You should also comment on the viability of each of the optional approaches, perspectives, ideas, and opinions in terms of their strengths and their limitations. Through your commentary on these approaches, perspectives, and opinions you are building a case for your conclusions and recommendations. You do this as objectively as possible, but as you do so evidence for your own choices could become apparent. You are building an evidentiary base for your conclusions and recommendations.

Use formal language in discussing these approaches and opinions, citing, from your sources, the pros and cons of each one. Be sure that each approach or opinion is discussed thoroughly. Use citations from literature reviewed, personal communications, and interviews as you build evidentiary bases for your commentary. You need to remember that you are providing, in this section, a strong evidentiary base for your conclusions and recommendations. When this section of your white paper or formal report, you are ready for the final section which consists of conclusions and recommendations.

Conclusions and Recommendations

This is the last section of your formal paper or white paper. If you have a number of conclusions and recommendations, you can separate them into two parts. These are the part of the paper where you bring together everything you have presented about current practices, perspectives, and opinions to develop and present your conclusions and recommendations. You have investigated the issue or problem from many perspectives. Your purpose was to inform a specific audience about a defined issue or problem. You know your audience and you need to consider the needs of your audience as you develop your conclusions and recommendations. Your conclusions are based on the evidence you have built in the previous sections of your formal paper or white paper. If the evidence is strong and specific and illuminates the issue or problem, your conclusions and recommendations will be sound and functional. Your readers, by the time they come to this section of your report or white paper, should have a clear concept and understanding of your conclusions and your recommendations will be. The audience knows you have defined the problem and discussed the background and current issues, Your audience understands the evidentiary bases, and become comfortable with the conclusions and recommendations.

This section is brief. You simply state what your conclusions and your recommendation in language similar to this: "Based on the review of current practices and opinions, I have concluded that. . . ." You use the same language for recommendations: "Based on the review of current practices and opinions and on my conclusions, I recommend that. . . ."

You may come to more than one conclusion and more than one recommendation. List them sequentially. Do not comment on nor embellish either the conclusions or the recommendations. If you have thoroughly written the background and current practices, perspectives, and opinions sections soundly and clearly with evidence and specificity, you will only need to list your conclusions and your recommendations. When this section is completed you have finished your formal paper or white paper. Congratulations.

Remember that you must follow the APA format and style. You are writing a formal report/white paper and you write it within the parameters of formal writing conventions. Use only the past and present perfect tenses in all sections of your paper. You may write the conclusions in present tense, though present perfect tense is acceptable. Follow all the grammatical expectations of formal writing. Use an economy of expression. Say only what needs to be said. Write predominantly in direct declarative simple sentences. Check the sections in this *Handbook* which deal with with these issues. Make sure the paper reads well. One way to ensure this is to read it aloud. You will hear, as you read, any writing problems in the paper. You should also have a reader to react to it and assist you in finalizing the content and the writing. The length of a formal report or white paper depends on the nature of the problem or issue, the audience for which it is written, and the purpose of the paper. You may divide the paper into the sections noted earlier. Instead of introduction, the full title of the report or paper is provided. The next sections are titled background, current practices and conclusions and recommendations. In most instances you will not need to include a table of contents. For longer reports and white papers you may want to include a table of contents as well as a review of literature as major sections of the paper. If you need a review of literature, you must have at least two level two headings with appropriate content. If level three headings are needed, you must have at least two with appropriate content. Be sure to refer to those sections in this *Handbook* if they are required or expected for your report or white paper. All works cited in the paper must be included in the reference section. For a quick review of the expectations for writing formal reports or white papers, refer to the checklist on page 139.

Preparing a Guidebook or Handbook

14

You may, in your professional career, be assigned to write a guidebook or a handbook. The purpose of a guidebook is to provide for the reader a step by step process for putting together a product, delineating a process, or developing a set of directions for how to do a task or series of tasks. A guidebook or handbook consists of a sequential series of steps developed to instruct readers on how to complete a task, learn a process, or achieve the objectives described sequentially in the purpose of the handbook. A guidebook or handbook is generally written in narrative form with each step in the sequence explained thoroughly, clearly, and as succinctly as possible. A guidebook or handbook should serve an identified audience and should include clear, sequential, and specific directions for the process of developing a product, learning a process, or completing a task. It may also contain illustrations or pictures to visually refer to some steps or to each step in the process. There is a slight variation in purpose between a handbook and guidebook. A handbook is sometimes more focused on providing information about a topic rather than on the sequential process to complete the process. We refer to them interchangeably here.

> A guidebook or handbook is generally written in narrative form with each step in the sequence explained thoroughly, clearly, and as succinctly as possible.

Organization

You should provide for the readers an introduction in which you explain the purpose of the handbook and introduce the materials needed and why they are important.

Back up information and references could also be included in your guidebook. References are placed in a reference section immediately following the narrative. Back up information should be included in appendices so they will not impede the process, but would be available to the reader for more detailed information. Appendices are placed at the end of the handbook following the references. They can be referred to in the guidebook.

You must write your guidebook or handbook clearly and concisely with each step clearly explained. This economy of expression and clarity of language are essential in preparing a guidebook or a handbook. Many guidebooks or handbooks fail because the language is too technical or too obtuse. In these instances readers do not easily follow the guidebook and can become confused about the process. Readers should not have to struggle to interpret your directions and the sequential steps. A guidebook or handbook is not designed to illustrate your technical knowledge nor your sophisticated and esoteric language. It must be clear, cogent, and concise. Your guidebook or handbook will usually contain a table of contents that follows the guidelines in this *Handbook* (pages five and six). The table of contents includes a listing of all categories or steps and, if needed, subcategories or sub steps. It also can contain a list of all materials needed to complete the process.

Additional support information and directions are placed in appendices. Appendices contain information and specifics too detailed to be included in the guidebook or handbook. Your appendix will include supplementary material related to the process outlined in the guidebook. All materials in the appendixes are keyed to specific steps in the guidebook or handbook and provide necessary backup material or information for the users. Information in the appendixes, like narrative materials in the handbook itself, follow APA guidelines and are written, for the most part, in the past or present perfect tense. Conventions of formal grammar and formal writing conventions are followed in preparing your guidebook or handbook. If needed, you will include a reference section following the narrative in the guidebook or handbook. References are those resources cited in the guidebook and in the appendix. In the appendix additional information and evidence will be provided for the readers so they can gain a more complete understanding of the product or the process.

Writing Tips

Your handbook should follow the conventions of formal writing in most instances. Sometimes a slightly less formal language can be used dependent on the topic or process. The APA format is however, the standard used in preparing your guidebook. Adaptations should be made carefully, but the core of the writing should conform to APA. This is especially true of professional audiences. It is important that you write clearly and concisely in providing directions and steps in the process. Use short declarative simple sentences in your narrative. Follow the conventions of formal grammar. Make sure that, in the appendixes, you provide a clear explanation of backup materials necessary for interpreting sequential steps and for a better understanding of each of the steps. Sometimes in writing guidebooks or handbooks there is a tendency to assume a certain level of understanding in your audience. Make no such assumptions. The language must be clear, be concise, and easily understood. The vocabulary can be adapted to the audience, the format cannot. The steps must be sequential with logical transitions from step to step. To ensure that you have completed all components expected within the handbook, refer to the checklist on page 140.

15 Preparing a Staff Development Program

Preparing a staff development program is a professional activity and responsibility. Staff development or professional developments begins with a needs assessment and includes identifying outcomes, determining personnel needed and their roles, gathering resources, developing a specific plan for the program, sequencing activities, involving participants the activities, and evaluating the outcomes. These are the essential components of preparing a staff development program and must be thoughtfully considered and carefully planned to ensure the success of the program.

 ## Needs Assessment

Before you actually begin specific planning of your staff development program it is wise and usually necessary to do a needs assessment to determine both the interest and skill level of the participants in terms of the content of the staff development program. A needs assessment can help you learn what the participants feel they need, and the kind of outcomes they expect from the staff development program. A needs assessment should be a straightforward questionnaire or survey designed to determine level of knowledge and skills in the area of the proposed program. A five or six point semantic differential scale or Likert scale could also be used as part of the survey to determine knowledge and levels of

> *A needs assessment should be a straightforward questionnaire or survey designed to determine level of knowledge and skills in the area of the proposed program.*

achievement. Skills to be included in the program could be listed along with participant's level of knowledge and understanding included in the semantic differential. Outcomes about what the attendee would expect to learn in terms of the objectives should be included in the survey. It is wise to put a copy of the needs assessment in an appendix.

It is important to keep the survey relatively brief. The survey should, if possible, be no more than one page in length and should be easy to complete. The format should be inviting and attractive. It needs to be distributed at least several days before the staff developed program is scheduled. In this way you will have time to very specifically plan the staff development based, for the most part, on the needs assessment. The analysis of the survey results is integral to the planning of the staff development program. In the final evaluation of the staff development the survey and the analysis of the results should be included in an appendix following the evaluation report.

 ## Identifying Outcomes

Analysis of the survey or questionnaire needs to be thoughtfully and carefully done. This analysis is vital to planning for the success of the staff development program. You cannot really plan goals, expected outcomes and the skills developed during the program without careful analysis of the needs assessment survey or questionnaire. After the analysis of the needs assessment the planning process begins with identifying the expected outcomes of the program. The outcomes should be specific, written clearly, and focused on the real or perceived needs of the participants. Differentiated outcomes need to be considered based on the responses to the needs assessment. Differentiated outcomes need to be listed along with processes for their achievement. The planner first needs to consider the needs of the participant and their perceived outcomes of the staff development. Once this has been done you should relate those stated needs and those expected outcomes to your planning of the outcomes of the staff development program. Based on perceived needs and expected outcomes, those participating in the staff development activities may need to have differentiated instruction and participative interaction. Planning should incorporate the need for differentiated areas of focus and differentiated outcomes where necessary. Identifying outcomes requires thoughtful and careful consideration of the information gained from the needs assessment.

 ## Personnel

The question of selecting personnel for the staff development program is an important component of the overall planning process. You need to develop a list of people who will organize the program, present the program, fill support roles, ensure that materials needed are identified and in place, develop sequences of activities, be responsible for involving participants, do the evaluation, and fill ancillary service roles. Include job descriptions where necessary. All of these kinds of roles must be considered in your pre-planning. Depending however, on the number of participants and the kind of activities included, most or all of these roles could be filled by a few individuals. For larger numbers of participants and a large number of activities, you may need multiple personnel for some or many of these roles. Your identification and placement of participating personnel should be based on the needs assessment and on your definition of the expected outcomes of the staff development program.

Organizing the Program

This is primarily the developer or leader's responsibility. You may, however, wish to delegate this responsibility to another person. Within this organizational process you need to outline the components of the program and put into them as much detail as needed. Design any workshops within the program as well as any specialized differentiated activities to meet the needs of the participants. Develop time frames for each activity and the content of each component. Make sure you plan for transitions, breaks, as well as snacks, lunch, or dinner. You need to carefully build a sequence of activities that will build toward an effective conclusion and a strong evaluation. All of this information should be written into your planning narrative for the program.

Presenters

Presenting personnel are very important to the success of the program. It is essential that strong presenters be selected to lead all workshops in the program. You should review the qualifications of possible presenters and check on how they have done in previous presentations on the subject. If possible, it is wise to choose respected members of the company or school district to which participants are assigned. These presenters are often known to the participants and have either the authority of leadership or the professional respect of the participants. If the presenters possess both, so much the better. If you have workshops or hands on activities built into the presentation you need to get the best people possible to lead those interactive groups or workshops. Selecting peers, when possible, is a good way of providing such leadership.

Plan for an evaluator or an identified person to be responsible for evaluation. Evaluation consists of a summary or review of the program that could be done interactively with participants. Then the participants complete an evaluation form. The evaluator should attend the large group formal presentation, walk through and observe small group activities and workshops, and interact with participants wherever possible. The evaluator summarizes the program, which can be presented or discussed interactively with the participants. The evaluator distributes and collects the evaluation forms. The leader and the evaluator are then responsible for the analysis of the evaluation form and the preparation of a final report. You may also want to include the presenters, the activity/workshop leaders, and other personnel in the preparation of the final report. All personnel involved in the program need to provide an assessment of the quality of their participation and the completion of their roles.

In addition to the professional presenters, workshop/activity leaders, and evaluator, there are other personnel roles to consider. You need to determine who will register the participants, who will set up the areas or locations for all activities, who will decorate the activity areas if needed, and who will ensure that snacks, lunch, or dinner are prepared and served. You will need to identify those who are responsible for any technology and other materials needed for the program and who is responsible for set up and removal of materials. You will also need to identify human resources to deal with equipment breakdowns, spills, health issues, and emergency procedures. Including all of these personnel issues is essential to the success of the program.

Resources

You should make a list of necessary resources needed for the program. This will include technology resources, print resources including handbooks and support materials, supplies and equipment for workshops or activities, writing pads and pens/pencils for taking notes, and other resources that may be needed for ensuring the success of the program. Be sure these are all in place by the beginning of the workshop. Seating arrangements and areas for small group activities need to be determined.

Planning for Differentiated Needs

From the needs assessment you have found that there have been a number of needs expressed by participants. These expressed needs may require differentiated approaches. You should prepare to meet those needs by designing activities and workshops in small interactive group settings where participants an raise questions and discuss issues. This is very important if you wish to have participants have an optimum learning experience. There could be a series of activities or workshops through which participants could be involved. If, for example, you plan three activities for each participant these could be arranged in an hierarchical progression designed to meet the needs of identified participants.

Involving Participants

For most staff development programs it is important to involve participants in a variety of differentiated activities and/or workshops. You need to plan for small group focused activities or workshops. You need to make them, in many instances hands on interactive group settings with defined activities. They could also be discussion groups. You could even have the activities involve both discussion and hands on. Participants need to have an interactive context in most staff development programs. If participants can leave the program with some kind of product, it can be a real plus for the participants. Interactive involvement with defined outcomes leads toward a more positive evaluation.

Evaluation

Evaluation, as already noted, should be a defined personnel position. The leader or program coordinator may fill that role. As the coordinator and developer you may select another person to fill this role. The evaluator should attend all large group sessions, visit each workshop or activity, interact with as many participants as possible, ask questions, and take notes. The evaluator should be on the program as the last presenter. The evaluator should review the presentations, the workshops/activities, and provide some of the comments obtained earlier by interaction with the participants. These comments should, for the most part, be positive. In some instances the comments from participants could touch on ideas for follow up programs, how to use the material learned, and what were the most valuable parts of the program.

After the summary presentation that could also be done interactively, the evaluator then introduces the evaluation form. The evaluation form could include an overall evaluation of the program using a semantic differential. It could also include checklists on what elements of the program could be implemented or used by the participants. The most valuable components of the program and what might be changed if the program were to be used again could be included. Each workshop or activity in which the participant was part of the group should be evaluated. This could be done either at the end of the program or at the close of each of the activities. The evaluation form should be kept as simple as possible.

Keep the evaluation instrument to one page if you can. Be sure it is anonymous, although some demographic data such as department, school, or assignment could be incorporated at the beginning of the evaluation form. You, the evaluator, and other identified personnel should be responsible for gathering the results of the evaluation instrument and writing the final report of the program.

Writing Tips

When writing your staff development program you need to include information about all of the components listed above. You are writing this staff development program in narrative form. In writing your report on the program you follow the conventions of formal writing. You use the past or present perfect tense for the most part. In describing processes and expected outcomes you may use other appropriate tenses. You follow the APA guidelines for formal writing as well as using this *Handbook*. Your report should be clearly and concisely written. All written documents should be reviewed, edited, and finalized.before the program is scheduled to begin. In your report you will address each of the components of the program and discuss each. You will include results of the evaluation form for each component of the staff development program. Each of the components could be a category for your report. Remember to use an economy of expression. If the report is lengthy, prepare a table of contents. Be aware of the audience for the program. It could go only to supervisors, managers, and to executives of the company or school district. A report needs to provided for the participants. It can be an abbreviated report or it can be the full report. Participants need to have all or the parts of the evaluation report pertaining to participation and identified outcomes. You, as developer and coordinator of the program, can make that choice. It is good to inform participants, in some way, the results of the evaluation. Strongly consider this as a part of your evaluation report. You can choose to share the whole report or parts of the report. For a quick review of the components of staff development programs see the checklist on page 141.

16 Preparing a Program Evaluation

Every program, project, theme or unit, and intervention needs to be evaluated. You can do an evaluation through qualitative or quantitative research or you can evaluate programs, projects, units, and other interventions through an identified process. The focus in this section of the *Handbook* is on evaluation through an identified process, although there is a category in this section on research. Program evaluations are usually required by the corporation, by the school district, or by program managers. If state or federal government entities or a foundation has funded the program or project, program evaluations are almost always specifically required.

Overview

Evaluation is the process of reviewing a program to determine its effectiveness and to determine whether it should be continued or terminated. This is a necessary process and one which is sensitive because it involves personnel, stakeholders, and the company, school, or school district in which the program is functioning. There are two kinds of program reviews. One is done by personnel within the company, the school, or the school district and is called an inside evaluation. The second is called an outside evaluation and is done by evaluators not associated with the company, the school, or the school district.

> *Evaluation is the process of reviewing a program to determine its effectiveness and to determine whether it should be continued or terminated.*

There are two major kinds of program reviews. There is the program quality review designed to determine the quality and value of the program. In addition, there are compliance reviews which could also be done from within the company, the school, or the school district or they could be done by outside evaluators. Compliance reviews are designed to determine whether the program is following the foundation, state and federal guidelines required by the funding source. Compliance reviews are required by most funding sources. Private funding sources can also require compliance reviews.

Because compliance reviews are specific to the funding source, they are not central to this work. The focus here is on program quality review. Funded programs usually have a designated time frame ranging from one year to up to five years. These kinds of program reviews are done annually beginning with the first year. Programs that are funded by the companies or by school districts generally follow the same or similar evaluation processes.

In many instances, program evaluations are done by a team of evaluators. On the team there is usually a lead evaluator and with other members of the team who may specialize in particular aspects of the program being evaluated. The evaluators work as a team and develop strategies, sequences, and activities for the evaluators. They study the program, identify the expected outcomes, review the processes involved, and develop the written program evaluation. They interview participants, observe the program in action, review written materials from the project. In some instances in funded programs with limited budgets, the evaluation is done by a single evaluator, often from the project itself. In those instances, the evaluation form and process is defined by the funding source. For our purposes we are considering only those evaluations involving a team.

Background Information

Before the program evaluation actually begins you and your team, as evaluators, should receive the initial funding proposal and any annual reports about the function and results of the program. Be sure to require all annual reports from the inception of the program. These reports should include program benchmarks and objectives, a detailed budget, program timelines and activities, personnel, tests and evaluation measures, and results of those tests and evaluations. Evaluations and program outcomes are particularly important. The most recent program evaluations are essential to the evaluation process. Also needed are program goals and objectives for the next year along with a projected budget. Program managers should, in addition, provide you with a list of stakeholders including employees, consultants, parents, students, members of the board of trustees, or advisory councils, and any others that may be pertinent to the operation of the program. If you are evaluating for a corporation, stockholders should be included as being stakeholders. Be sure to contact the program managers and identify the information you and your team will need. Discuss the time frame for the evaluating the program and the components of the program. Program information and evaluations, particularly from the most recent year, are essential for conducting the evaluation.

The timeline for the evaluation needs to be developed before the evaluation begins. Identify the components and plan for time frames for each. Time should be allocated for an open meeting with program managers and personnel, observations of operations or classroom observations, and interviews with program managers, program personnel, participants, and stakeholders. Questions should be prepared for interviews. Identify what needs to be seen in the observations. Time for writing and preparing the final report also needs to be included in the timeline. As noted, be sure to discuss the timeline with program managers and make any adjustments related to schedules that may be needed. Do not leave out any of the components noted because of scheduling problems. Remember that most program evaluations generally take more than one day. Plan schedules for the time needed. Generally major program reviews take about three to four days.

Steps in the Evaluation Process

After you have completed your timeline, contacted the program managers, and have made any adjustments necessary, the evaluation process can begin. When you and your team arrive, you first meet with the program managers and finalize the schedule for the program review. Hold an open meeting to share this information, discuss the process, and indicate the time for the final meeting. Respond to any questions. You may make minor adjustments in the evaluation process through such a meeting. After the open meeting observations take place. This is followed by interviews with program managers, personnel, and stakeholders. At the close of each day the team should meet to share notes, discuss issues, and work on the preparation of the final report. Discussion should focus on the strengths of the program, identified limitations, and the relationship of what is observed and interview results in the context of program objectives. In the second and third day this process continues with the progressive writing of the final report. On the final day of the evaluation the final report is completed and presented during an open meeting including program personnel, participants, and stakeholders.

Writing the Final Report

Because you are writing a report that will be publicly heard and usually read verbatim, you need to consider the writing process carefully. The formal and final report should include a brief statement about the nature of the program and how it has developed and changed from its inception. It includes the objectives of the program and progress toward the achievement of those objectives. Generally you are evaluating during the actual implementation of the program and where it is at that time in its development.

Yours is not an end of year report. That is done by the program managers and is reported to the funding source. Your report should reflect the actuality of what was observed, the feelings and attitudes of the managers, personnel, participants, and stakeholders. You will report the strengths of the program and the positive elements within it. You will also define limitations and areas that need to be changed or improved.

The final report is both a process and a product evaluation of the program. You note the processes followed and the outcomes achieved. Your evaluation report is a critique of the program from the perspectives of your team. Much of it will be positive, yet the report needs to include recommendations for change and improvement. You will develop a rich, thick narrative of what you observed, your interviews with managers, personnel, and stakeholders. You can include pertinent comments from your interviews when they are pertinent and appropriate for the report.

You then, from the evidence provided, develop conclusions and make recommendations. Generally these will be positive, but within them you can conclude that certain things within the program need to be adjusted or changed. In the report you then recommend a process for making those changes. These conclusions and recommendations are what the program managers, personnel, and stakeholders have been waiting for. When you write these, they should be carefully wrought, but straightforward and to the point. It is your task as evaluators to give a sound professional judgment as to the quality of the program and make suggestions for changes and adjustments to improve the program. It should be noted that you may cite sources to provide additional evidence for your conclusions and recommendations. These citations can be placed in any section of the report as long as they are pertinent and do not impede the clarity of the report.

You should also meet with program managers daily to ensure that you are gathering all the necessary information, seeing all the important activities, and interviewing stakeholders pertinent to the program. The program managers need to be informed about your process and any questions you and your team may have. They need to keep you and your team well informed and provided with any information the team may need. Always plan to review the final report with the program managers before it is read publicly. This is important because the managers need to know what is being presented. They may even suggest editorial changes if time permits. They may also provide responses to the recommendations that can informally be presented at the open meeting if appropriate.

In the open meeting the report is usually read verbatim by the reviewers to ensure that there is no mistake or misunderstanding by the audience. Copies of the report may be made for the program personnel or stakeholders. After the report has been presented, the program managers may want to make a brief statement. Allow for this. Thank the managers, the personnel, and the stakeholders for their participation in the evaluation and then allow for questions. The time for questions is usually relatively brief, but all questions should be addressed. Additional questions can be referred to the managers and personnel who can, at a later time, receive your responses to the questions.

Writing Tips

We have briefly reviewed the process and have discussed the writing of the report. It should be remembered that the APA format and style should be followed. Your report should have these sections: Program summary, program objectives, program operations and personnel, and conclusions and recommendations. These are the categories you will consider. You may title them differently depending on the program. You may write your formal paper or white paper as a narrative without the use of formal categories. In doing so, however, you need to include the sections noted above. Be sensitive to the needs of your audience and utilize the most effective organization you can to meet those needs. You will also want to include in the program summary a brief history of the program. You will include pertinent citations and follow the narrative with the reference section. Write clearly and concisely and use an economy of expression. All listeners need to be able to understand your report and how it pertains to them. Adjust the vocabulary of the report, as needed, to accommodate this need for understanding. Use, for the most part, simple declarative sentences. For a quick review of the components of program evaluation see checklist on page 142.

Preparing a Grant Proposal

Grant proposals must be developed according to the guidelines and format of the request for proposals (RFP). These are provided by the funding source. In the RFP there is an expectation for a statement of need, the goals and objectives of the proposed program, a time line for the implementation and achievement of those goals and objectives, a budget for funding the proposed program, and personnel necessary for program operation. Each RFP will have these basic components. Additional components, information and legal requirements would be specified in the RFP.

Preparing a Grant Proposal

In preparing your grant proposal you would first specifically describe the problem or issue being addressed and the interventions you are proposing. You will need to define the problems, the need for change, and the importance of the interventions. You will specifically note the needs addressed and how the interventions relate to the identified needs. To do this you may need, if space permits, to cite sources that both substantiate the need and identify the importance of the interventions. This must be done specifically and in some detail so that the readers of the proposal can clearly understand what your problems are and how you are going to intervene to address and resolve the problem. You must use an economy of expression and say only what needs to be said.

> Grant proposals must be developed according to the guidelines and format of the request for proposals (RFP).

You will also need to prepare broad program goals which clarify program purpose and support the interventions planned. Goals are broad general statements of outcomes. Goals are your generic expectations. They should be supported by specific measurable objectives that are keyed to each of the needs you have already stated. The measurable objectives should be directly related to a timeline during a designated time of program operation. Benchmarks, processes, and identified products and outcomes should be fitted into the timeline so that readers can clearly note the sequence and process involved in the program. This is important because readers need to be able to easily identify the objectives and the timeline and be able to understand the process involved in the program interventions. Within this process, an evaluation plan needs to be in place.

It is important to identify personnel needed to operate the program. Personnel could include managers, support personnel, certificated personnel, and classified personnel. Where necessary job descriptions or personnel roles could be provided. Personnel information should be included in the appropriate section of the narrative expectations within the RFP. You should note the stakeholders in appropriate categories of the RFP. Stakeholders could include those served, parents, and the community.

Budget Preparation

You will need also to prepare a budget for your grant proposal. Budgets for education project usually include seven categories: First (1000), a category for certificated personnel. Second (2000), a category for classified personnel. Third (3000), a category for benefits such as social security and workmen's compensation. Fourth (4000), a category for supplies and equipment. Fifth (5000), a category for operational costs. Sixth (6000) a category for capital outlay such as computers and technology. Seventh (7000), a category for indirect costs such as electricity, rent, and custodial services provided by the district or company. These categories may be slightly different if you are writing your budget for a company or corporation. Your company or school district usually charges a fixed percent for indirect costs. These are most of the components of a budget. Budgets not specific to education may have a slightly different set of budget categories. Your RFP will provide specific guidelines for budget preparation.

Compliance Issues

Be sure to carefully review the RFP for compliance issues that you will need to address. Include any other requests for information such as demographic data and inclusive dates of the program if designed for multi year operation. Include any additional information that may be needed by the funding source. Among this information should be demographic data relating both to program personnel and program participants. Compliance issues are very important to the successful grant proposal. These are the basic components that need to be addressed when writing a grant proposal. It is wise to have your grant proposal reviewed by others who will be associated with the grant to ensure clarity and logical development.

Writing Tips

Your first obligation is to follow the requirements and categories of the RFP as they have been identified and defined in the document. You need to follow the directions within each category very specifically. For narrative portions of the grant proposal follow the format and guidelines of the APA. Syntax is very important in grant proposals. You must use, for the most part, short declarative sentences in the active voice. Be straightforward and honest in what you say. Make sure that the language is clear and that the elements and narratives in the grant proposal are logical in their progression and follow each other sequentially both in terms of narrative and the completion of the material required by the funding source. Remember that you will have other professionals competing for funding. Your proposal must follow the conventions of formal writing and the expectations of the funding source. Best wishes. For a quick review of the expectations for grant writing see the checklist on page 143.

18 Preparing an Action Research Study

Chapter

Action research refers to an individual preparing and conducting a research study with a small population. The population could be one person or it could be up to thirty or more. Action research is generally qualitative research, though it could be quantitative or a combination of both research paradigms. Essentially action research involves a manager or a teacher who develops and implements an intervention with people in a defined group. Action research can be done with one person or one student. When this happens, action research can also be termed a single case research study.

The general purpose of action research is to find out how an intervention works with a relatively small group of people or students. Preparing an action research project is somewhat less structured than a formal qualitative or quantitative study. There are, however, some parameters within which the researcher must work. In writing an action research project you must first clearly enunciate the purpose of the study including objectives and expected outcomes. Second, you need to identify the need for and the rationale for the action research. Third, you need to identify the intervention clearly and succinctly. Fourth, you need to specify how you plan to implement the research and prepare an activity timeline for the study. Fifth, you need to provide an evaluation design to show how you are going to determine the outcomes or results of the intervention.

> *The general purpose of action research is to find out how an intervention works with a relatively small group of people or students.*

Purpose

You need to clearly state the purpose of your action research. The reader needs to know this at the beginning of your action research proposal. You, as the researcher, must be very clear about this and specifically state it. An opening statement such as: "The purpose of this action research study was to. . . ." Then specify your purpose and add the objectives of the action research. Objectives need to be measurable and either behaviorally oriented or involve changing a process, changing attitudes, or utilizing the learnings from the planned intervention. The objectives may vary somewhat depending on whether this is a single case research study or involves a somewhat larger group. The purpose and the objectives are very important components of your action research. State them clearly and succinctly.

 Rationale

Early in your document you need to identify the rationale for research. You need to tell the reader why you are doing the research. The question of why the research is needed is one you should answer early in your action research proposal. The need for the research must be apparent and substantive. The rationale could have two dimensions. First, the importance of the topic in the field needs to be stated. Second, the importance of the topic to the population involved. The perspectives on rationale need to be explained and at least one needs to be included in your document. You may focus on the more localized of the rationales, or on the wider importance of the topic to the field. You may even include both of them in your document. You need to cite some sources for your rationale and for your intervention. Include a reference page for resources you have cited. For action research you do not necessarily need a review of literature. You do, however need to cite pertinent resources in the field that relate directly to the question addressed in the study.

 Intervention

Your intervention needs to be clearly and succinctly stated. The intervention needs to be defined and linked to the purpose of the research, to the rationale, and to the stated objectives of the study. You need to be clear and concise in your definition of the problem and provide information about how the intervention will be implemented, monitored, and administered. Here again you also need to cite resources in order to support the professionalism of the intervention. Your intervention needs to be sound, as simple as possible, and be designed to meet the objectives and the identified needs. If necessary, you could include a small budget request for materials or other incidental expenditures.

Implementation

It is important to define implementation in terms of process and activities. You will need to provide an expected timeline for each activity. You will need to address the process of implementation and any differentiation in the intervention as the research progresses. A timeline of the components of the intervention activities needs to be developed and followed. Adjustments could be made as necessary based on participant responses to the interventions. It is important to identify benchmarks and link evaluation strategies to the the implementation and associated timeline. In many instances, particularly in single case action research, you need to keep an anecdotal record of what happened during the implementation. In larger studies you need to observe events, define and discuss changes in the participants, and keep accurate and objective records about the process of implementation and change. Implementation is the centerpiece of your action research and you must keep accurate records about how the process was implemented, noting the activities and benchmarks, and recording the results of the activities resulting in benchmarks.

 Evaluation

Your should, in your action research, have a well defined evaluation design. You may use observation and anecdotal records. You may also use pre tests and posttests. You could interview participants and you could use a survey or questionnaire. You could use performance-based tasks or creation of defined products. There are, of course, other evaluation strategies that could be used. You need to select those most pertinent to your research. Regardless of the evaluation design, you should use it in a way that will demonstrate to the reader what changes occurred through the intervention. If you used tests, surveys, or interviews the results will give you and the reader a perspective on the effect of the intervention. If you are using a survey, you can use descriptive statistical measures to determine outcomes. Descriptive statistical measures most generally used on action research are mean, median, mode, range, and standard deviation. If you feel comfortable with other measures such as inferential statistical measures or correlational statistical measures, use them. They are not, however, generally used for action research. If you use anecdotal records, they must be complete and provide the necessary detail to indicate the impact of the intervention on the participant(s). Evaluation is very important and the results need to be shared and publicized. This is especially true if you want to have the intervention replicated by others. Do not neglect to write conclusions and recommendations for your action research study.

Once these five steps have been accomplished, you have completed your action research study. Action research is something a professional can do. You can do it in your department or in your classroom You can use action research with one person or with a group of people. Action research is something a manager or teacher can do without depending on consultants of any kind. Inform your supervisor, obtain permission to do the study, identify what you want to do, plan specifically and sequentially, and follow the steps described above. Implement confidently, keep track of what you do, have a strong evaluation plan, and determine the results of the intervention carefully. Consider whether your action research could be replicated. If so, write a thorough report and share it with company or school district personnel.

Writing Tips

Action research is less formal that qualitative or quantitative research. It is done on a small scale and with limited personnel. When writing your action research proposal, you need to follow APA guidelines. Write crisply and cogently. Use short declarative simple sentences for the most part. The past tense and present perfect tense should be used most of the time because when you write the report the research has been completed. You will be citing some sources, even though you do not usually have a review of literature. Be sure to follow APA guidelines for these. Include a references page. It is important to use an economy of expression. Make every word count and choose the right word to illuminate meaning. Your purpose is to tell the story of your research clearly and concisely, but with enough detail to make it a professional representation of what you planned, what you did, how you did it, and the results achieved in your study. For a quick review of the expectations for preparing an action research study see the checklist on page 144.

19 Preparing a Personal Response Paper

A personal response paper is developed as a professional response to an issue or problem in an identified field. A personal response paper is not a polemic, it is a measured and thoughtful response to the topic, problem, or issue you have addressed. It follows as specific organization and format and is consistent with the APA. It contains four sections including the introduction, a background to the problem including history and review of literature, next is the discussion, and finally there are the conclusions and recommendations. They are frequently included in the discussion section.

Introduction

The introduction follows the title page and the abstract. Both of those are consistent with the APA. The introduction begins with the title as it appears on the title page. That title may be a statement of the problem or issue followed by a colon and then the words "a personal perspective" or "a personal response." This indicates that the paper will reflect your points of view. It will be objective in its development, but in the end, it is your reflection about the issue or problem. After the title you will state the purpose of the paper. The purpose of the paper generally is to investigate the issues, look at a variety of resources that demonstrate opinions and views on the problem or issues. The purpose of the paper should also reflect the parameters of the paper including a specific focus on issues related to the problem. You then tell why the topic is important. You will need to cite some sources in defining the purpose of the paper. Do not cite too many resources. That is for the next section.

Background Information

The next section of a personal response paper is designed to provide a background to the problem or issue. It requires a review of literature specific to the topic. It can be titled background information, review of literature, history and background, or history and current points of view. This section should include what scholars, commentators, and experts in the field have reported and presented in research studies or publications. A history of the problem or issue should be included in a personal response paper to illustrate how the issue has been viewed in historical contexts. Any research results or relevant information about the issue or problem need to be included in this section. This section needs to be a thorough review of literature as well as a review of the history, background, and development of perspectives on the issue or topic. Be sure to include as many different perspectives and points of view that you can find in the literature. They should be included in your background section. This history and review of pertinent commentary and recent studies becomes the core background for the paper and a presentation of various points of view about the topic. It must be done carefully and thoroughly. It should clearly demonstrate your understanding of the issue from a variety of perspectives and from a wide variety of resources.

From an organizational perspective you should divide this section into level two and level three sub sections or categories as needed. The content included in heading levels two and heading levels three can provide organizational support for you and thus can help the readers understand the organization and sequence of your background information. Remember that you must have at least two categories. If you use subcategories, you must also have two subcategories.

 Discussion

The next and generally the final section of the paper is the discussion. This section is titled discussion. This is really the heart of your paper. It is only in this section that you present your ideas and views. Sometimes conclusions and recommendations are contained in a fourth category. That can be done to emphasize your personal conclusions and recommendations based on your points of view. It is this section of your paper that you are able to present your responses to the issue or problem. It is the only section in the paper where these points of view and personal responses are presented. The discussion section contains these categories: Summary, interpretation, conclusions, and recommendations. What you do in this section of the paper you are building a case for your conclusions and recommendations about the issue, topic, or problem. You have four things to do. First you summarize what you have presented in your background and history of the issue. Next, you interpret that material. Third you develop conclusions, and finally you make recommendations.

Summary

In this section you summarize the information you presented in the background information or review of literature. You do this as succinctly as possible. Note only the most important and salient points that you brought forward in your background and history section of the paper. It is important that you cite many points of view in this summary, even those with which you disagree. This summary information should include only citations from resources you have used in your paper. You should present this summary objectively. Report only on what was said by the authors of your resources. What you use in the summary you must use in the next category of this section. The sources in the summary are those that link the interpretation category to the summary.

Interpretation

The interpretation category is the key to the presentation of your personal response. This category of the discussion is where you can begin to share your ideas and perspectives. It is in this interpretation category of your personal response paper that you build your case for your conclusions and recommendations. Here you are expected to agree and disagree with specifically named resources and show their points of view about the issue. After you have presented several points of view, you need, through your interpretation of the the issue, to begin to focus on particular resources with which you agree and build a logical case for that approach to the issue. Remember, though, that you can only use resources used in the summary. The reader needs to refer back to that information and not have to reread the whole background section to find the context.

Your interpretation must be done forthrightly and honestly as an expression of your personal opinions, interpretations, and responses to the issue or problem. The interpretation is actually a presentation of your ideas and your approach to resolving the issue or ameliorating the problem. It is within these contexts that the whole thrust of your personal paper gains credence and viability. It is vital to the purpose of personal response papers that you do this convincingly. Again, you are not writing a polemic. You are writing a reasoned and thorough response to an issue that has been studied from many points of view and you are synthesizing those points of view in your interpretation. It is not emotional and you should avoid the use of any words or terms that can hint at bias. Just build your reasoned analysis into a synthesized and well-evaluated person reaction to the issue. In this way you are building a case for the conclusions and recommendations you will be making about your current feelings and perspectives on the problem or issue. These final statements in the interpretation level three heading section must be carefully wrought and presented logically and sequentially to make your case clearly apparent to the reader.

Conclusions

What you have written in the interpretation should validate the conclusions and recommendations you make here. Conclusions and recommendations drawn from the interpretation constitute your last level three heading section. This can be one level three section if you have few conclusions and recommendations. The level three heading section would then be called conclusions and recommendations. It can be two level three heading sections if you have several conclusions and recommendations. With two level three heading sections they are named conclusions and recommendations as the second level three heading section. In your conclusions and recommendations you make specific the conclusions you have developed. You do not need to explain or elaborate in your conclusions. You have done that in the interpretation category. Just write them as succinctly and clearly as possible. A sentence like "based on the background information and the literature reviewed, I have concluded that. . . ." can be used to state the conclusion. The conclusions should be written in simple sentences. Write them as briefly and succinctly as possible. Use only only enough words to ensure clarity of meaning. Your conclusions should stand alone as the summative expression of your personal response to the issue or problem. It should be clear to the reader, through the conclusions, your perspectives and response to the issue. Additional conclusions are written in the same manner.

 ## Recommendations

Recommendations are statements about what you feel should be done, changed, or implemented based on your interpretations and conclusions about the problem or issue. Recommendations are based only on your interpretation, your personal response to the background and literature reviewed, and on your conclusions. Recommendations, like conclusions, should not be lengthy nor complex. Like the conclusions, the evidentiary base should be drawn from your the background information and literature reviewed. They should also reflect your interpretation and response to the issue or problem in the discussion section. Recommendations should be correlated with the conclusions. Recommendations should be written in the same manner as shown in the conclusions statement. Personal response papers almost always need recommendations. For personal response papers this is the final narrative statement of your paper. Do not go into an elaboration or seek to explain our recommendations. Do not add any new material. State what you recommend. State it clearly and succinctly. It should be straightforward and carefully written. These kinds of recommendations can bring a strong closing to your paper and be the final representation of your personal response to the issue or problem.

Writing Tips

It should be noted that you will follow APA and formal writing conventions in a personal response paper. You need to use past tense or present perfect tenses in your paper except in the interpretation. There you may use present tense. In your recommendations you may use present tense or, in some cases, future tense. All headings, the level two section, and level three subsections should be written consistent with APA. Remember not to use personal pronouns in the abstract. You may use personal pronouns in noting why you chose the topic or issue. You may also use personal pronouns in the interpretation, the conclusions, and the recommendations. Use them sparingly and only when needed. Write clearly using, for the most part, simple declarative sentences in the active voice. Avoid anthropomorphisms and other common errors in writing. Your writing should be objective and reasoned. Your personal responses should not be evident until the interpretation section of the discussion. The checklist for personal response papers can be found on page 145.

20 Writing for Online Courses

In this section of our work we focus on how to write for online courses. Online course writing, while it follows certain format and style require- ments, in our case APA; it does have expectations and elements of writing different from on site courses. In this section we point out those differ- ences and how to adjust to them. While the writer is expected to follow formal writing conventions, there are parameters and expectations for online writing that differ from on site classes. Among those parameters and expec- tations are word expectation for assignments, time frame for assignment completion, threaded discussions, chat sessions, and communication among students as well as communication between instructor and students, and evaluations. We will briefly mention blogs and wikis, but they are not the real focus of this section of our work.

Parameters and Expectations

Writing for online courses is an exercise in clear and cogent writing with parameters. Among those parameters are the word expectation for each of the assignments. You will find within the course a minimum word expec- tation for each assignment. That word expectation is found in the syllabus under the weekly assignments. At our institution that word expectation is generally 1,000 words. Submitting fewer than the expected minimum will cost you points. Instructors have computers that provide a total word count. Remember that the word expectation for the assignment does not include title page, abstract, or references. The assignment should always meet the assignment word expectation.

Another parameter is the time frame for the assignment. You have an designated date and time when the assignment is due. Keep to that schedule. Do not deviate from it. Late assignments can cause loss of points. If you are ill or have an emergency, you must e-mail the instructor. In some instances the instructor will grant you an extension. Let the instructor know when you will finish the assignment and submit it by that time. If you do not communicate your need for an extension to the instructor, you will lose points for late submission.

Threaded Discussions

In most online courses there is a discussion component. For these discussions, some-times called threaded discussions, there is a prompt based on text readings or other designated material. The student is expected to prepare a response to the prompt and to respond to another student's post. The initial student response should include citations from the text, required readings, designated material, or other sources. Follow the citation format in APA or your institution's style manual. Students should use direct quotes when appropriate. List the resources used at the end of the response. While dis-cussions are written in less formal style than are the assignments, the writer must be careful about spelling, and grammar. Be particularly careful about capitalization. Over capitalization has been a frequent error in threaded discussions. It is a general expec-tation that students should respond to one or more than one other student posts.

The instructor also participates in the discussions. Generally the instructor will respond to initial posts. The instructor may also add new ideas or different perspec-tives. Students should respond, where appropriate to the instructor's posts. The pur-pose of the threaded discussions is to engender thinking and interaction. Student participation is essential. On point to remember is that discussions are not just responses to a prompt. They are interactive learning experiences in which students and the instructor exchange ideas about the stimulus in the prompt. The discussions are specifically keyed to the defined outcomes of the course and add a dimension of inter-change of ideas which is so important in online teaching and learning.

Chats

Chat sessions are generally scheduled by the instructor. Students are invited, at a desig-nated time to discuss the course, review writing expectations, explain and elaborate on the assignments, and other topics pertinent to the course. Chats are most frequently done in writing with the instructor and the students writing commentary as well as asking and answering questions. Chats should be done within a designated time frame. The longest time frame we have used is an hour. That time can be extended if needed. Chats should remain focused on the agenda for the session. The agenda, while generally planned by the instructor, can be suggested by the students. Be brief, concise, and clear in your chat statements. There will be typos and errors. Generally avoid comment on them. Stick to the agenda until the agenda is complete. Then there may be more personal comments in the closing moments of the chat. Students and instructors enjoy this time of interchanging personal data, discussing family and hobbies, or chatting about sports and other interests. These times can be very important because they show the personal side of the participants in the chat. These are good interactive times.

It should be noted that chat logs could be read and reviewed if some class members could not join the chat session. It is strongly recommended that students read the chat logs to gain information that has been provided during the chat. In that way the students who were not in the chat can have the same background information about course expectations, writing formats, and specific assignments. All students will need to have the information and expectations discussed in the chat sessions whether they participated or not.

The instructor may want to have small group chats with a few students to discuss issues or problems pertinent to them. The instructor contacts the students and sets up a chat session with them about how they are doing, changes they need to make, errors they need to eliminate, group projects or specific course content related to their assignments. Students may also set up chat sessions to work together on assignments, special projects, small group discussion or interpreting assignments or prompts. These kinds of small group chats are recommended for building rapport, solving problems, building projects, and sharing pertinent information.

Some chats can be done with programs that allow for voice interaction rather than typed chat information. This is a strong step forward in chatting and working with students online. It increases rapport and makes the chats both informational and personal. Instructors and students can also post pictures for chat sessions. This too helps to build rapport and provides a picture of the participants. In some instances video chat conferences can occur when both instructor and students have access to video cameras. Skype or similar video programs can be used for small groups of students. Any or all of these can and should be used when the technology is available. They dimensionalize chats and make them more interesting to both students and instructor.

Communication

It is essential that communication between instructor and student take place. It is also important for communication among students be in place. These communications help build interactive involvement and build relationships, establish rapport, build respect, and help students take responsibility for learning. Communication is done through a number of formats. Threaded discussions, chats, and e-mail are kinds of communication for the instructor and for the students. These are all done in writing. Writing in these kinds of communication should be clear, to the point, and express feelings and meanings with an economy of expression. It is essential that the instructor touches bases with students when that is needed. Students should feel free to contact or communicate with the instructor when there is a need to do so. One of the major purposes of online courses is to develop positive and open communication between the instructor and students and among students. Open and frequent communication energizes optimum learning in online classes.

Evaluations

For every assignment, paper, project or threaded discussion there is a designated point score. For every threaded discussion there are designated numbers of points. For group reports and course papers there are points to be earned. Points generally total 100 for all the work in the class. Sometimes an instructor may give extra credit for additional work, but that is not done often. The student is expected to turn in every assignment, participate in all threaded discussions, complete assigned projects, and any end of course project or paper that is required. The instructor will evaluate every element of the course that is keyed to course work and which has an assigned point designation.

For every assignment completed, there is an evaluation. The instructor will provide a written assessment and evaluation of student work. Those evaluations should be specific and detailed. They should note achievement and success, point out strengths, and define areas where improvement is needed. It is essential that the instructor write evaluations in detail. It is equally important for the student to read the evaluation statement of the instructor and make any changes needed for future assignments. This is the process to which both the instructor and the students must adhere. It is vitally important to teaching and learning online. Students can learn to correct errors and instructors can clarify, explain, or elaborate on topics, issues, or problems. Students should feel free to respond by e-mail and discuss the evaluation with the instructor. One point; do not make the same mistake over and over in any assignment or course activity. It will cost the student points and it will irritate the instructor. Students can monitor their point scores as the course progresses.

Podcasts and Video

A podcast is a voiced commentary on the course or on ancillary material. A podcast posted online by the instructor, a student, or a small group of students. First there must be a script. It must be carefully and specifically written to focus on the topic or issue pertinent to the class. Written scripts for an online course need to follow formal writing procedures as noted in this *Handbook* unless there is a different genre or less formal writing style approved by the instructor. The instructor or students read the script into a microphone and post the verbal presentation on the course document sharing area. A podcast can be heard by the students and they can download the podcast. A podcast can add a verbal dimension to the course that can be a real asset to students. Background music, pictures, and other visuals can be added to the podcast. Student response to podcasts has been very positive. Podcasts can be used to augment communication and interaction between the students and the instructor, provide new information for the class, or respond to an assignment or a prompt.

It should also be noted that visuals and videos presentations could be posted for student use. Video and even dialogue can be used within the video. Videos also begin with a script that relates to the course. Video presentations prepared by the instructor or students can also be a strong support for course content. In addition they can provide supplementary materials for students to see and hear. Students can gain more information about issues and areas of discussion within the course through these video presentations. They, along with podcasts, can be used as prompts for chats and discussions. They can bring in additional dimensions of content into the course.

Blogs and Wikis

It is not our intent to go into detail about blogs and wikis. We do want to note that, in some instances, they are part of online teaching and learning. Blogs are posted in an online site with direct links to the course. Blogs are generally posted for a longer period of time than threaded discussions. Students respond to the blog with personal perspectives on the statement in the blog. As students respond, those responses are listed sequentially. Blogs are designed to build on the comments posted. As such, they are focused and sequenced. Each comment should be designed to build on previous comments. As blog comments are made definition and points of view are added to and enlarged. Thus a blog can become a learning experience for student within the course context. Blogs can be assigned points for course evaluation, but generally that is not the case.

Wikis are generally linked to concepts or issues within the course. Wikis are posted online with links to the course. They are initially most frequently posted by the instructor, but on occasion, students can post wikis. A wiki is designed to be edited. It can be changed and further expanded and developed. Wikis are a collaborative work on the part of the participants. It can be used to build consensus about issues in the class. Whenever it is changed, the name, time, and date of the student making the change are posted. Wikis provide an interactive format for participatory involvement. They can be enlarged and become a source for student reference. Wikis, like blogs are not usually a part of course work. We must, however, be aware of them. Blogs and wikis are a part of the growing online interaction and in the future may become a part of online teaching and learning.

Writing Tips

For assignments within the course work, the student must follow APA. The student is responsible for preparing a title page, and abstract, pertinent and quality content, and an abstract. Each one of these components must follow APA. Abstracts should be written in past tense. Content within the assignment should for the most part use past tense and/or present perfect tense. Write in simple declarative sentences for the most part. Do not use personal pronouns in your abstract or in your paper unless you have a conclusion or recommendation. Refer to this work or to the latest edition *Publication Manual of the American Psychological Association* for specific help in writing. In sum, assignments require strict adherence to the conventions of formal writing.

Writing in threaded discussions is less formal than assignments. Students should be careful about spelling and capitalization. Rules of grammar and syntax should be followed. Cite sources and reference them at the end of your discussion post. Chat and e-mail should be written carefully. In chats there will be errors in syntax and spelling, but these can be ignored. E-mail should be carefully written and you should avoid colloquialism and slang. It is, however, less formal than in the assignments. If the student has a written project or formal paper as a culminating work for the class, then all elements of formal writing conventions and the format suggested in this work should be followed explicitly. Writing online is both similar to and yet somewhat different than writing for an on site class. Writing is, however, the core element in successful online teaching and learning. The checklist for writing online is on page 146.

21 Preparing Curriculum

Creating or developing a curriculum, while focused on education, can be applied to any instructional sequence required for new employees, for retraining, or for developing new skills for groups of people. There are a number of steps involved in preparing curriculum. Among these are selecting standards, identifying objectives, creating a time frame, deciding what classroom structure to use, determining primary materials for the curriculum, choosing technology if needed, determining the level of cognition to be achieved, identifying teaching strategies, deciding on assessment practices, and developing an instructional sequence. If you have members in your class who have a home language other than English, you will also select identified specially designed activities in English (SDAIE) as well as providing for a reflection or review of how the lessons worked with the students. Each of these level two or three heading sections is defined and explained in this narrative.

First, however, you will need to prepare an introduction to the curriculum in which you note the purpose of the curriculum unit, theme, or area of focus. In the introduction you will also need to identify the importance of the curriculum. Here you may cite some sources and follow the style and format of the APA for those citations and for the narrative. The final component of the introduction is the rationale for preparing the curriculum. Why you chose it and why you detailed the specific area of focus or content. These three items complete the introduction. You will

You should be familiar with the standards in your own state and use them for planning your own curriculum.

also need to have a title page for the curriculum. For the introduction and the title page follow the instructions in the *Handbook*. You may need to include a table of contents in the curriculum package. Again, follow the instructions in the *Handbook*. In this work, we have presented a format for curriculum development. You can use it or you may be expected to follow a school district or corporate format. Use this format as a model and adjust it to meet district or corporate needs.

 ## Selecting Standards

Standards are provided for schools in every state. One state calls them learning expectations. In a more generic sense, standards provide the expectations for students to be able to demonstrate when the curriculum is completed. If you are teaching in a school you need to be aware of the standards provided by your state department of education. Performance standards or performance expectations are also used by companies or other institutions to reflect minimum skills needed for certain jobs or activities. Those are the standards a company, an organization, or corporation will be expected to achieve. You will need to select a standard for each instructional lesson. Sometimes more than one standard can be selected. However, usually one standard can be used for each lesson. In a longer sequence of lessons, several standards could be used. Remember that standards remain constant for a designated period of time. They are the expectations toward which you are working in terms of your instruction. In education there are standards for every grade level and for every content area. There are slightly different formats, names of content areas, and structures in each state. You should be familiar with the standards in your own state and use them for planning your own curriculum.

 ## Identifying Objectives

After you have selected the standard or standards you are working toward, you need to identify the specific objectives for the lesson or lessons you are teaching. Your objectives should be behavioral and skill oriented. This means that within the objectives behavior outcomes are noted and skill objectives are expected. Behaviors, skills or processes should be noted in the objectives. Objectives should be brief and to the point. They should reflect what you feel the outcomes of the lesson should be. You may use only one objective or you may include more than one objective for a specific lesson. In writing your objective, conceptualize what you want the students to learn, to be able to do or demonstrate, or what they will be able to build or create. Take real care in preparing your objectives. They are essential to the success of your lesson. It is always important for students to be aware of both the standard toward which they are working and of the objectives they are expected to achieve by the end of the lesson or lessons. If you have a series of lessons on a particular topic, plan objectives for each lesson.

They should be linked together and built on each other. In cases where there are a series of lessons, objectives can change based on the results of each lesson. Objectives could change depending on how students have reacted to individual lessons. Lessons later in a sequence of lessons may need to be changed as students learning is demonstrated. Some skills, for example, may need to be retaught. Be prepared to make any necessary changes in objectives.

Time Frame

In your planning consider the time it will take to achieve the objectives you have planned. Each individual lesson should have a time frame ranging from a few minutes to a period or even to a workshop of one or two days. You need to gauge the amount of time needed for the students to demonstrate that they have achieved the objective or the measures implied in the standard. Approach the time frame thoughtfully. If there are a series of lessons related to specific objectives, note how much time is needed and for how many periods or days are needed in the sequence of lessons. Sometimes the time frame is dictated by the schedule of allocated time in terms of periods or a specific beginning and ending time. You need to develop the time frame keeping within any parameters and ensuring that you will have enough time to achieve the objectives in your lesson or lessons.

Classroom Structures

Classroom structures indicate how you are going to organize for teaching. There are many ways to structure your classroom. You can use whole group instruction through direct instruction followed by large or small group activities, or you may use a wide variety of group structures. Some group structures that could be used include pairs, triads, cooperative groups, dialectic groups, jigsaws, and many others. Steinaker and Leavitt (2010) identify many group structures, define them, and show how they can be used in the classroom. You can also use a combination of structures. For example you may wish to start with whole group instruction so that students will gain some basic knowledge of the subject and be introduced to the standards, the objectives of the lesson, study, or workshop. You can also provide any basic information the students need including a time frame and schedule. Following whole group instruction, you may wish to break the class into cooperative groups or other kinds of group structures. Groups can be assigned the same task or each group can have a different assignment. You make the choice. Groups should be carefully planned, have defined tasks, and be monitored and sustained by the teacher or by assigned assistant teachers. When group work has been completed or when the time frame for group work is completed, the class can be called together for sharing, discussing, arriving at a consensus, and evaluation. You have real flexibility in planning your classroom structures. Choose those you feel will work best for the participants.

Primary Program Materials

You will be using specific materials for your lesson or lessons. You need to note the materials you will be using with your students/participants. Among the materials you could use with your students are district adopted basal materials or textbooks. You may also use trade books or supplemental texts. You may use newspapers, journals, or magazines. Artifacts, realia, or hands-on materials can be used. Handbooks or guidebooks can also be used. In many instances you could use audiovisual materials or computer programs. You need to select those materials that would be most helpful to you and your students in achieving the stated objectives of the lesson or lessons. Select the materials carefully and be sure that you can access and provide the materials. Make sure there are enough materials to serve all your students. You need to make sure the materials can be read and understood by the students or participants. Wherever possible you should review the materials and become familiar with them before you use them with students or participants. Understand when they will be used in the lessons, why they were chosen, how they relate to the lessons, and how they will be used.

Group Structures

You need to consider how you will group your students during the course of the lesson. There are many group structures you can use. You may even use more than one group structure in a learning session, depending on the nature of the lesson. Group structures can be whole group instruction, cooperative learning groups or a number of other group structures. Among the other group structures are pairs, triads, numbered groups, single focus groups, planning groups, jigsaw groups, and dialectic groups where two or more ideas or points of view are given. Then the group comes to a consensus about the perspective they feel is most appropriate. There are other group structures that you can use (Steinaker & Leavitt, 2010). We want to emphasize the value and importance of interactive learning through group structures. It is through interactive group learning that students become engaged and where learning is augmented and optimum learning becomes possible.

Technology

Technology is a tool for learning, but in the context of many schools, districts, and business organizations it is a vitally important tool. You need to select the primary technology you will be using along with other support technologies. Among the technologies you could use are computers, keyboards, overheads, slide projectors, film projectors, compact disks, video disks, calculators, television, radio, podcasts and programs like Skype where you can do video conferences and conversations with another person or a small group of people. There are other technologies that you and the students could also use. Students can create films, prepare podcasts, develop power point presentations, and use technology to learn content. Instructors may use more than one technology in the program or in the lessons. When using technology, the instructor should explain how it is used and how it relates to the objectives of the lesson or lessons. If participants are to use the technology, be sure they know how to use it and can function well with it. Provide any assistance or support that may be needed.

 ## Cognitive Levels

In any lesson you need to be aware of the levels of cognition and your expectations for students to achieve as high a level of cognition you have planned for the lesson or lessons. There are seven levels of cognition. They are memory, translation, interpretation, application, analysis, synthesis, and evaluation. For memory an objective can be written using these terms: Defines, identifies, names, describes, lists, and remembers. For translation the operant words are matches, grasps, tells, understands. Interpretation means explaining or summarizing, interpreting material, predicting outcomes or effects, and estimating future trends. Objectives at interpretation can be written using terms such as convert, defend, distinguish, estimate, explain, generalize, rewrite, give examples. For application students use material in new concrete situations and apply rules, methods, laws, and theories. Words for objectives at application are changes, computes, uses, demonstrates, solves, shows, operates, applies. Analysis means breaking into parts, organizing materials to establish criteria, clarifying and drawing conclusions. Descriptors for objectives at this level of cognition are breaks out, outlines, discriminates, subdivides, compares, organizes, distinguishes, diagrams, relates, and contrasts. Synthesis relates to preparing a unique communication, developing a set of abstract relations, and putting parts together for a new whole. Words used for writing objectives at synthesis are combines, composes, compiles, creates, designs, rearranges, modifies, develops. The highest category of cognition is evaluation. Here students judge value based on established criteria, supports judgment with reason and evidence, and values for specified purpose. Terms used for writing objectives at evaluation are appraises, critiques, judges, chooses, supports, values, selects, evaluates.

A single lesson should reach the application level of cognition. In a series of lessons you may have lessons in each cognitive level and each lesson should be planned to move the students toward the higher levels of cognition.

Teaching Strategies

Teaching strategies are the methodology of instruction. You will need to select teaching strategies that will help ensure student/participant learning. Below we list twenty-five teaching strategies with brief descriptors. For a complete definition of these teaching strategies see Steinaker and Leavitt *Interactive Learning: The Art and Science of Teaching* (2010). Please note the descriptors are not written, in some cases, as complete sentences. The specific strategies and their descriptors are as follows:

Goal setting: Establishing relationship to previous learning, introducing the lesson. Establishing set and objective.

Data presentation: Providing information, establishing stimuli, identifying resources, using media.

Directed observation: Focusing on particular or selected stimuli, establishing lesson parameters, identifying what to look for.

Data exploration: Student and teacher interacting with the data. Identifying how to find information. Checking for understanding and readiness for next steps in the lesson. Often done interrogatively.

Reflective modeling: Teacher models processes involved in the lesson and interactively with students established clear vision of outcome and how to get there. Students identify relationships to previous learning and respond to known examples.

Generating/using data: Accumulating appropriate resources, generating data, reading, viewing, listening, discussing. Using "why questions, examining additional data.

Unstructured role playing: Providing for role playing and interactive unstructured modeling of student perspectives on the experience. Asking students to show relationships, show a process, or play a role pertinent to the lesson.

Use of manipulatives/realia: Using and exploring realia (hands on artifacts). Involvement in hands-on activities. Learning how to use materials.

Ordering: Sequencing data, arranging data, establishing material hierarchy, defining frames of reference, preparation for guided practice. Also involves checking for understanding.

Selection of data: Selection of needed data and resources for guided practice activities. This strategy is focused use of materials. Reading, viewing, working with others.

Using/interpreting data: Using assessing, interpreting data through observing, reading, viewing, and experimenting. Recording data, explaining.

Discussion/interaction: Exchanging information and points of view, questioning, information giving, clarifying. Interaction between teacher/students and students/students. Cooperative groups are appropriate in this strategy.

Hypothesizing: Conceiving and using provisional assumptions as the basis for reasoning and action. Conjecturing possible outcomes or possibilities. Developing hypotheses, identifying processes and possible results.

Testing hypotheses: Trying conditional hypotheses in many situations. Applying data, asking questions, confirming or rejective hypotheses, processes, possible outcomes.

Using acquired skills: Use of acquired information and skills. Applying information and skills to problem solving. Demonstrated achievement of lesson objectives.

Observing/sharing: Reviewing processes and sequence of lesson. Sharing, discussing, using and demonstrating learned skills or behaviors. Can also be done in written format or in multimedia form.

Role playing/simulation: Structures role playing. Overt demonstration of learned skills and roles using simulation, discussion of outcomes and sharing achievement and success.

Comparing/contrasting: Applying learned skills to new contexts. Analysis of similarities and differences in these new contexts. Can be interrogative and/or interactive.

Summarizing: Reviewing the lesson. Identifying the sequence and process. Developing ideas for reporting and sharing with others.

Reporting: A written, graphic, or multimedia sharing, showing, or explaining the lesson to others.

Presenting: Showing, sharing the experience and its value. Teaching others the processes involved.

Dramatizing: Preparing a skit, play, demonstration. Formalized presentation of the lesson.

Instructing/teaching: Interacting with others about the meaning of the lesson. Can involved peer teaching.

Evaluating: Interactively assessing the meaning of the lesson in terms of developing ideas for new lessons. Looking back on the whole experience, valuing it, and determining new experiences.

These teaching strategies are organized hierarchically. Each five teaching strategies correlate with levels of the interactive taxonomy (Steinaker & Leavitt, 2010). Those levels are invitation, involvement, investigation, insight, and implementation. You should select several strategies and key them to specific activities in the lesson sequence. Plan them carefully and use them during the delivery of your lesson.

SDAIE Strategies

Specially designed activities in English or SDAIE are strategies and activities instructor uses for students whose home language is other than English and who did not do well on English language development tests. They are also good strategies for any learners and can be used with all students. There are many SDAIE strategies. Among them are:

Clustering/semantic mapping: Accessing prior knowledge, reviewing lessons or unit. Using a pre reading activity (clustering). Reviewing a lesson, assessing comprehension (Semantic mapping). A post reading activity.

Cooperative learning: This is also classified as a teaching strategy. A variety of group structures can be used.

Directed reading-thinking activity (DRTA): A pre reading activity involving an interactive dialogue about a story including predicting, reading, discussion, review of predictions, application and analysis.

Found poem: Using a work of literature, document, an original work to help students develop and define personal meaning and interpretation.

Advance/graphic organizers: Organizing information visually. Visually organize and contextualize language. Needs to be used in conjunction with direct instruction.

Introducing students with material to help them learn vocabulary and content in a lesson.

Guided reading: Introduction of reading material including new vocabulary. Discussing story and making predictions.

Interactive writing: Focusing on particular skills in writing, phonics, spelling, grammar, punctuation, editing, revising.

KWL: Focuses students on what they are learning. Students list what they *know*, what they *want* to learn, and on what they have *learned*.

Language experience: A student centered method that uses student language as a basis for reading and writing. Good for all students.

Oral patterned responses: Students respond or generate dialogue using a particular pattern (choral reading, reader's theater).

Print rich environment: Meaningful text posted around the room that students use for information and vocabulary.

Reader's theater: Teacher or student narrates story as students act it out. Choral reading and student developed skits can be used.

Role playing: Students dramatize situations or stories. This is also classified as a teaching strategy.

Selective listening and "cloze" procedure: Using procedures to check on comprehension and vocabulary. Used to reinforce writing skills. Includes partnering and small group activities.

Shared reading: Teacher and students share reading a story, poem, rhyme, or chant.

Shared writing: All students contribute to the writing a group story. Individual students contribute their own sentences or words.

Think-pair-share: Used in all content areas. Students are to *think* about the question or problem, *pair* up with a partner, and *share* their answers with partner and class.

Writer's workshop: Collaborative approach to the writing process. Students spend time writing and conferencing. Teacher comments on student writing and provides encouragement. Writing is shared and teacher works with students to bring writing to publishing stage.

These are some of many SDAIE strategies. There are many more. We have provided only brief descriptors of the strategies. We have listed only the most commonly used strategies. When planning a lesson, you need to consider SDAIE strategies and incorporate them in the lesson plan. They are also good strategies that can be used for any students and not just for English learners.

Assessment

Assessment is integral to the success of the lesson. The teacher and the students need to know how well they have learned. Assessment is really the capstone of the lesson plan. Assessments are both short term and long term. Long term assessments are normative tests and criterion referenced tests (CRT). Shorter term assessments are running records (usually for reading and language arts, but could be used in any content area), writing samples, end of chapter or unit tests, demonstrations, use of an oral reading rubric, multimedia reports, teacher made tests, skills tests, and other evaluations. Other evaluations could be observation, interactive discussions, quality of created materials and realia, performance assessments, or group reports. You may use one assessment strategy, but usually you will use more than one strategy. Carefully plan the evaluation measures you will use. Whenever possible have the students demonstrate a learned skill. This can be done in a number of ways including some of the assessment strategies noted above. You should include process evaluation as well as product evaluation. Process evaluation deals with the process of the lesson and the process of learning. It is very important for the instructor and the students. The purpose of process evaluation is to improve the learning process and make it more efficient. Product evaluation deals with the quality of the outcomes of the learning experience.

Instructional Processes/Outcomes

It is in this category of lesson planning that you prepare a sequence of activities or steps you will follow in the course of the lesson. Each step needs to be delineated and sequenced for clarity of meaning. You may want to share the steps or sequenced with the students so they are aware of the direction of the lesson and your expectations for the achievement of certain benchmarks at specific steps. Be as detailed as is necessary for this sequence of activities. Do not leave out any step or make the steps so broad that they could be interpreted in more than one way. You may want to note how this lesson fits in to a unit of work or an instructional theme.

This is the lesson map. Follow the directions you have established in your planning. Share those directions with the students/participants so they also know expectations and the series of steps. You and they will navigate this process together This is a vital step and makes the lesson more viable for you and the students. Adapt this format, as needed, to meet district or corporate guidelines and format.

 Reflection

In many lessons (hopefully most or all of them) you will want to reflect on and evaluate what happened in the lesson delivery and what happened in terms of both the process and the achievement of the defined objectives. Did the students achieve the defined objective? Will the skill or process need to be retaught? What parts of the lesson might need reteaching? Were the teaching strategies, SDAIE strategies, and classroom structures appropriate for the lesson? Were the assessments sound? What strategies went right and you will want to use again? These are some of the questions that you may need to consider as you reflect on the results of the lesson. Reflection can also be a basis for next steps and next lessons. It is important that you reflect on your own instruction. This process can be of great use as you seek to become more effective as a teacher.

We have presented a very detailed and specific process for planning, delivering, and evaluating lessons. You need to use something like this for your lesson planning. Two good works that will help provide additional information on lesson planning are Serdyukov and Ryan *A five star approach to lesson planning* (2008) and Steinaker *Heuristic electronic lesson planner* (2007). A third source for lesson planning and analysis can be found in Seinaker and Leavitt (2010), *Interactive learning: The art and science of teaching*. For a quick review of the lesson planning process see the checklist for writing curriculum and lesson plans on p. 147. There are a number of lesson planning formats. You will need to use a lesson plan format approved by your instructor school district or supervisor. One lesson planning format which includes most of the categories in this curriculum guide can be found in Steinaker and Leavitt *Interactive learning: The art and science of teaching* (2010).

When writing curriculum you use complete sentences in every component where writing is expected. Your introduction is one such component. Be sure that the narrative included in your written plan follows the APA format and style. Refer to the appropriate sections of this *Handbook* for specific directions on organization and writing. In some instances you check off or list teaching strategies used, SDAIE strategies used, specific assessment strategies, and in other categories as well. Write clearly and concisely. Use short simple statements because you may want to share this curriculum with your students. Several of the categories will only require one word or brief responses such as cognitive level, classroom materials, time and date of lesson, and technology. Your lesson plans should be easily understood both by those who review your plans and by your students with whom you use the plan. Make sure, in particular, that the sequence of each activity is clearly and concisely written. This component of the lesson plan is one of the keys to a successful lesson. It needs to be written clearly, specifically, and succinctly. Be sure that you have a supervisor's approval for your lesson plan format. Finally, make sure that your lesson plan, in all categories noted, is complete and can be clearly understood by reviewers and students. The checklist for writing curriculum is on page 147.

Chapter

22

End Note

You have now completed a formal paper or project. This is one of several you will do in your graduate work and in your professional career. The exercise of formal writing is integral to your professional growth and to the development of your professional skills. As you grow professionally you will be expected to communicate your ideas, your perspectives, and your skills through writing as well as through speaking. Much of your written communication will be through formal writing. Formal writing skills help you in organizing, sequencing, interpreting information, drawing conclusions, and making recommendations. The utilization of these skills will be a strong asset in the development of your professionalism. Their use will also provide a basis for your growing perspectives and philosophy about your profession. Every strong leader needs to develop these qualities.

Be sure to keep your formal papers. A collection of these papers can be useful for reference and focus on issues, opportunities, and problems that may be a part of your professional assignment. The references you used for your papers can be a quick guide to obtaining sources and information. The bibliographies you have developed through your papers, particularly those with annotated bibliographies, can be a real asset to you professionally. Keep all of these. Wherever possible organize them topically so you can access sources on a particular issue. As part of your professional development, these papers, the references, and the bibliographies you have collected

> *Formal writing skills help you in organizing, sequencing, interpreting information, drawing conclusions, and making recommendations.*

can be very useful. Professionalism includes keeping current on issues and topics in the field. You should continue to read and reflect on these and add to your bibliography and sources as you continue your personal program of professional development. The acquisition of professional skills and experience can help you achieve you own personal professional goals. Congratulations on completing your paper and on your continuing development as a professional.

References

American Psychological Association. (2010). *Publication manual of the American Psychologial Association* (6th ed.). Washington D.C: Author.

Bennis, W. G. (1993). *An invented life: Reflections on leadership and change.* New York, NY: Addison-Wesley.

Bennis, W. G. (2000). *Managing the dream.* Cambridge, MA: Perseus Books Group.

Bennis, W., & Goldsmith, J. (2003). *Learning to lead* (3rd ed.). Cambridge, MA: Perseus Books Group.

Carver, R. P. (1984). *Writing a publishable research report in education, psychology, And related disciplines.* Springfield, IL: Charles C. Thomas.

Cone, J. D., & Foster, S. L. (1993). *Dissertations and theses from start to finish: Psychology and related fields.* Washington, DC: American Psychological Association.

Darling-Hammond, L (1997). *The right to learn: Blueprint for creating schools that work.* San Francisco, CA: Jossy-Bass Education Series.

Drucker, P. F. (1967). *The effective executive.* New York, NY: Harper and Rowe.

Eisner, E. W. (1994). *The educational imagination on the design and evaluation of School programs.* (3rd ed.). New York, NY: Macmillan College Publishing Company.

Gall, M. D., Borg, W. R., & Borg, J. P. (1996). *Educational research: An introduction* (6th ed.). White Plains, NY: Longman Publishers USA.

Howard, R. (Ed.). (1993). *The learning imperative: Managing people for continuous innovation.* Boston, MA: Harvard Business School.

Joyce, B., Weil, M., with Calhoun, E. (2004). *Models of teaching* (7th ed.) Needham Heights, MA: Allyn and Bacon.

Likert, R. (1967). *The human organization.* New York, NY: McGraw Hill.

Merriam, S. B. (1998). *Qualitative research and case study applications in education.* (2nd ed.). San Francisco, CA: Jossey Bass.

Mertens, D. M. (2004). *Research methods in education and psychology: Integrating Diversity with quantitative and qualitative approaches* (2nd ed.). Thousand Oaks, CA: Sage Publishers.

Reeves, D. (2003). *Making standards work* (3rd ed.). Denver. CO: Center for Performance Assessment.

Sample, S. B. (2001). *The contrarian's guide to leadership.* San Francisco, CA: Jossey-Bass.

Serdyukov, P., & Ryan, M. (2008). *A five star approach to lesson planning.* Boston, MA: Allyn and Bacon.

Steinaker, N. W. (2007). *Heuristic electronic lesson planner.* Trabuco Canyon, CA: Communications L. T. D. helplp.com

Steinaker, N. W., & Bell, M. R. (1979). *The experiential taxonomy: A new approach to teaching and learning.* New York, NY: Academic Press.

Steinaker, N. W. & Leavitt, L. S. (2010). *Interactive learning: The art and science of teaching.* (2nd ed.). Dubuque, IA: Kendall-Hunt Publishers.

Strunk, W. Jr., & White, E. B. (2000). *The elements of style.* (4th ed.). New York, NY: Allyn and Bacon.

Turabian, K. L. (2007). *A manual for writers of term papers, theses and dissertations* (7th ed.). Chicago, IL: University of Chicago Press.

Checklists for Sections of Formal Papers and Writing

In the pages that follow are a series of checklists. There is one for every section of the formal paper you are preparing. Also included are checklists for the table of contents, a bibliography, and appendixes. A generic checklist for conventions of formal writing is provided. Checklists for writing formal reports and white papers are included. In addition checklists for preparing a guidebook or handbook, staff development programs, grant proposals, action research studies personal response papers, online writing, and preparing curriculum are included. The checklist for formal writing should be used as the final check of your paper. Each checklist is designed for your personal review of the paper you have prepared as the writer. You can use these checklists both as you write and as a final review to determine if you have completed all the necessary components of each section of your paper or study. This is done to ensure that you have followed the formal writing conventions as well as the APA format and expected components of each section of the paper.

In addition, if you are a student writer, there is a signature form for you and for your instructor including the date when the checklist is completed and provided for the instructor. These checklists can also be used for conferences between you and your instructor or supervisor. Space is provided on each of the checklists for comments by you, by your instructor or by your supervisor. Page numbers referents are included to note the page number in the *Handbook* where the information needed to complete the each point on the checklist is provided. During the preparation of your paper, you may need to use several of the checklists more than once when you conference with your instructor or supervisor. If you are enrolled in a class, these checklists may be provided for you by your instructor. They can also be obtained through the publisher.

If you are writing your paper individually for submission to a specific audience or to a journal or other publication, these checklists are provided to ensure that you have followed the format suggested within the *Handbook* and are consistent with the APA. Be sure to use them because they provide you with a final check about your adherence to formal writing conventions and to the format outlined in the *Handbook*. Again, our best wishes to you as you use these checklists. We are sure that you will find them helpful. If you need additional copies of the checklists or the *Handbook*, please ask your instructor or your supervisor for copies. You may also contact the publisher.

Checklist for Preparing the Title Page

Directions: Please fill out the checklist below. Circle yes or no for each item listed. Make any comments necessary in the space provided. Page numbers following each item indicate the references to the page or pages where you will find the information about how to complete the item.

1. I have included a running head (1–2) .... Yes   No

2. I have provided the full title of my paper (2) .... Yes   No

3. My (our) name (s) as author (s) is listed below the title (2) .... Yes   No

4. I have included the author's affiliation (2–3) .... Yes   No

5. I have provided any other information expected by the instructor, the organization, or the group to which the paper will be submitted. (3) .... Yes   No

6. I have included a date of submission (optional) (3) .... Yes   No

7. All elements of the title page are centered as specified (1) .... Yes   No

Comments:

_____

_____

_____

_____

Writer's Signature_____

Instructor's Signature_____ Date _____

Checklist for Table of Contents

Directions: Please fill out the checklist below. Circle yes or no for each item listed. Make any comments necessary in the space provided. Page numbers following each item reference the page or pages on which you will find information necessary to complete the item.

1. Table of contents has a running head with only the short all in caps version of the title and numbered in lower case Roman numerals (5) .... Yes No

2. The table of contents immediately follows the title page (5) .... Yes No

3. Ellipses are correctly entered (5) .... Yes No

4. The title is centered and is in text (5) .... Yes No

5. Level two headings are justified on the left and are on a separate line (5) .... Yes No

6. Level three headings are indented two tab spaces (6) .... Yes No

7. Page numbers are justified to the right margin (6) .... Yes No

8. Appendixes are listed by title and page number in the table of contents (6) .... Yes No

Comments:

_____

_____

_____

_____

Writer's Signature_____

Instructor's Signature_____ Date _____

Checklist for Preparing the Abstract

Directions: Please fill out the checklist below. Circle yes or no for each item listed. Make any comments necessary in the space provided. Page numbers following each item indicate the reference to the page or pages where you will find the information on how to complete the item.

1. I have included a running head with only the capitalized short
   version of the title and numbered page two (7) . . . .   Yes   No

2. The word abstract appears as the title centered and in bold one
   double space below the running head (7) . . . .   Yes   No

3. My abstract is blocked (8) . . . .   Yes   No

4. My abstract contains between 150 and 250 words (9) . . . .   Yes   No

5. My abstract is accurate, concise, and specific (8) . . . .   Yes   No

6. I have included salient points from the review of literature (8) . . . . .   Yes   No

7. The abstract was written in the past tense (8) . . . .   Yes   No

8. I have included results of my research study (9)* . . . .   Yes   No

9. I have included conclusions and recommendations (8) . . . .   Yes   No

10. I wrote my abstract after other sections of the paper were
    completed (8) . . . .   Yes   No

11. No personal bias or opinion is included within the abstract (9) . . . .   Yes   No

*Research studies only.

Comments:

_____

_____

_____

_____

Writer's Signature _____

Instructor's Signature _____   Date _____

Checklist for Preparing the Introduction

Directions: Please fill out the form below. Circle yes or no for each item listed. Make any comments necessary in the space provided. Page numbers following each item indicate the reference to the page or pages where you will find information on how to complete the item.

1. I have included a running head with only the short version of the title in caps and numbered three (1–2) .... Yes   No

2. Full title of paper is given one double space below the page header (11) .... Yes   No

3. Purpose of the paper is clearly stated at the beginning of the paper (11–12) .... Yes   No

4. The purpose includes limitations of the topic, the area of study, questions or issues, and other information especially in research studies (11–12) .... Yes   No

5. Importance of the paper/study has been evidenced with citations (12–13) .... Yes   No

6. Citations reflect resource writer's views about importance of the topic (13) .... Yes   No

7. I have prepared my rationale for choosing the topic (13) .... Yes   No

8. Everything in the introduction except from direct quotes was written in the past or present perfect tense (13) .... Yes   No

Comments:

_____

_____

_____

_____

Writer's Signature_____

Instructor's Signature_____ Date _____

Checklist for Preparing the Review of Literature

Directions: Please fill out the checklist below. Circle yes or no for each item listed. Make any comments necessary in the space provided. Page numbers following each item indicate the reference to the page or pages where you will find the information on how to complete the item.

1. I have included a running head on every page of the review of literature (1–2) . . . . Yes   No

2. Review begins with a paragraph listing level two and three headings (16–18) . . . . Yes   No

3. Level two headings are on a separate line from text and are in bold (16–18) . . . . Yes   No

4. At least two level two and two level three headings as needed (16–18) . . . . Yes   No

5. There was no personal commentary in the review of literature (18) . . . . Yes   No

6. Level three headings are indented followed by a period on a text line (18) . . . . Yes   No

7. Sources for every new idea or information were in place (17–19) . . . Yes   No

8. Past or present perfect tense was used except in direct quotes (19) . . . . Yes   No

9. I have put quotation marks around each quote under forty words along with citation and page number (19) . . . . Yes   No

10. Quotes of forty or more words with no quotation marks were used (19) . . . . Yes   No

11. Quotes of forty or more words including page number were cited (19) . . . . Yes   No

12. Everything in the review of literature is double spaced (15) . . . . Yes   No

13. An evidentiary base for conclusions/recommendations was in place (20) . . . . Yes   No

14. If needed, I have included a closing paragraph (18) . . . . Yes   No

Comments:

_____

_____

_____

_____

Writer's Signature_____

Instructor's Signature_____   Date _____

Checklist for Preparing the Method Section

Directions: Please fill out the checklist given below. Circle yes or no for each item listed. Make any comments in the space provided. Page numbers following the item are the reference page or pages where you will find information about how to complete the item.

1. I have included a running head for each page (1–2) . . . .   Yes   No

2. I have made each of the topics listed as a separate category (22) . . . .   Yes   No

3. I have completed the question or issue section (22) . . . .   Yes   No

4. I have used the past tense or present perfect tense
   in this section (28) . . . .   Yes   No

5. I have noted limitations, variables, population and sampling
   process (22–25). . . . .   Yes   No

6. I have discussed the time frame and process (25–26) . . . .   Yes   No

7. Data collection, assessment, and evaluation are included (26–27) . .   Yes   No

8. Data analysis mode, either qualitative or quantitative
   is in place (26–27) . . . .   Yes   No

9. I have provided enough detail for clarity and understanding (28) . . .   Yes   No

Comments:

_____

_____

_____

_____

Writer's Signature _____

Instructor's Signature _____   Date _____

Checklist for Preparing the Results Section

Directions: Please fill out the checklist given below. Circle yes or no for each item listed. Make any comments in the space provided. Numbers following each item are references to the pages in the *Handbook* where you can find information about how to complete each item.

1. I have included a running head on each page of this section (1–2) ... Yes   No

2. I have obtained results in a quantitative study using descriptive statistics, inferential statistics, or correlational statistical analysis (30–32)* .... Yes   No

3. Results in a qualitative study include a personal interpretation (34)* .... Yes   No

4. I have presented the results in a clear and concise way (33) .... Yes   No

5. I have included figures/tables, as needed, to present and clarify results (32) .... Yes   No

6. I have written my results section in past or present perfect tense (35) .... Yes   No

7. The results are clearly and cogently written (33) .... Yes   No

8. There is no bias, interpretation, or personal perspective in this section (34) .... Yes   No

9. I have disaggregated data, as needed, for each variable in the results (30–31) .... Yes   No

*Select only one.

Comments:

_____

_____

_____

_____

Writer's Signature_____

Instructor's Signature_____ Date _____

Checklist for Review of Literature Paper Discussion Section

Directions: Please fill out the checklist given below. Circle yes or no for each item listed. Make any comments in the space provided. Numbers following each item indicate the page numbers in the *Handbook* on which you can find information about how to complete the item.

1. I have included a runnng head for each page in this section (1–2) ...   Yes   No

2. I have included a summary of the review of literature written in past or present perfect tenses (42) ....   Yes   No

3. I have used citations in the summary (41) ....   Yes   No

4. I have interpreted the literature carefully and clearly using present tense and the personal pronoun I (42) ....   Yes   No

5. I have provided an evidentiary base for my conclusions (42) ......   Yes   No

6. My conclusions are clearly and succinctly stated (42) ....   Yes   No

7. Recommendations are based on evidence, the conclusions, and are clearly stated (42) ....   Yes   No

8. I have expressed my personal views on the review of literature in the interpretation, the conclusions, and the recommendations (42) ....   Yes   No

9. My conclusions and recommendations were concise and clear (41–42) ....   Yes   No

Comments:

_____

_____

_____

_____

Writer's Signature _____

Instructor's Signature _____ Date _____

Checklist for Discussion Section of Research Studies

Directions: Please respond to each item listed below. Circle es or no for each item. Make any comments in the space provided. Numbers following the item are the reference pages in the *Handbook* on which you can find information about how to complete the item.

1. Results are provided and related to the review of literature (41) .... Yes   No

2. I have cited studies related to this topic in the summary (41) ...... Yes   No

3. Results of this study have been related to other research
   studies (41) .... Yes   No

4. I have presented my views of the results in the interpretation
   section (41) .... Yes   No

5. I have interpreted the review of literature in terms of the results and
   the content of the review of literature (42) .... Yes   No

6. The review of literature provided an evidentiary base for
   the study (42) .... Yes   No

7. Conclusions were clear and concise and were drawn from the
   review of literature and the results (43) .... Yes   No

8. Recommendations were clear and concise and drawn from the
   review of literature, results, and conclusions (44) .... Yes   No

Comments:

_____

_____

_____

_____

Writer's Signature_____

Instructor's Signature_____ Date _____

Checklist for Reference Section

Directions: Please respond to each item listed below. Circle yes or no for each item. Make comments in the space provided. Numbers following each item refer to pages in the *Handbook* where you can find information on how to complete the item.

1. References follow the APA style (45) .... Yes   No

2. References are alphabetized by author or title when no author listed (45) .... Yes   No

3. Internet pathways are listed without underlining and in black with an APA approved 12 point typeface (46) .... Yes   No

4. I have included a DOI number where necessary (46) .... Yes   No

5. Everything in the reference section is double spaced (45) .... Yes   No

6. I have listed only the sources cited in the body of the paper (45) ... Yes   No

7. References are hanging reference with succeeding lines indented one tab space (46) .... Yes   No

Comments:

_____

_____

_____

_____

Writer's Signature _____

Instructor's Signature _____ Date _____

Checklist for Formal Writing

Directions: Please fill out the form below. Circle yes or no for each item listed. Make any comments necessary in the space provided. Page numbers following each item indicate the reference to the page or pages in the *Handbook* where you will find the information about how to complete the item.

1. There are no agreement errors in my paper (50) .... Yes No

2. I have eliminated all anthropomorphisms from my paper (50) ..... Yes No

3. My citations follow the APA style (51) .... Yes No

4. I have eliminated colloquialisms, idioms, and slang expressions from my paper (52) .... Yes No

5. My ellipses follow *Handbook* guidelines (52) .... Yes No

6. I have not ended or begun any line in my paper with a hyphen (52) .... Yes No

7. My paper is justified on the left margin except for table of contents (53) .... Yes No

8. I have used specific and precise language in my paper (53) .... Yes No

9. I have eliminated most or all of the he/shes from my paper (50) ... Yes No

10. I have no comma splices, run on sentences, or fragments in my paper (55) .... Yes No

11. I have used that and who correctly (56) .... Yes No

12. I have used the appropriate tenses in all sections of my paper (56) .... Yes No

13. There is no plagiarism in my paper (54) .... Yes No

Comments:

_____

_____

_____

_____

Writer's Signature_____

Instructor's Signature_____ Date _____

Checklist for Appendixes

Appendices may not be needed, nor required for your paper or study. If they are, please fill out the checklist below.

Directions: Please fill out the form below. Circle yes or no for each item listed. Make any comments in the space provided. Page numbers following each items are referents for the page or pages on which you will find information needed to complete the item.

1. I have included a running head (1–2) .... Yes   No

2. Appendixes follow the references and the bibliography (if included) (47) .... Yes   No

3. Each appendix has a title (48) .... Yes   No

4. If more than one appendix is included they are lettered A, B, C, D and so forth (47) .... Yes   No

5. My appendixes include information pertinent to my paper or study (48) .... Yes   No

6. My appendixes are listed in the table of contents (48) .... Yes   No

7. I have referred to the appendixes as needed in sections of my paper (48) .... Yes   No

8. I have followed APA style and format for all appendixes (48) ...... Yes   No

Comments:

_____

_____

_____

_____

Writer's Signature_____

Instructor's Signature_____ Date _____

Checklist for Bibliography

A bibliography is not always required in a review of literature or a research study. If it is required, please complete this checklist.

Directions: Please fill out the form below. Circle yes or no for each item listed. Make any comments in the space provided. Page numbers following each item are referents for the page or pages on which you will find information needed to complete the item.

1. I have included a running head for the bibliography (1–2) . . . .   Yes   No

2. My bibliography immediately follows references and is on a
   new page (47) . . . .   Yes   No

3. My bibliography contains only additional resources related to
   my topic (47) . . . .   Yes   No

4. I have annotated each entry in the bibliography (47) . . . .   Yes   No

5. My annotations are blocked one double space below
   the entry (47) . . . .   Yes   No

6. I have followed APA for each entry into the bibliography (48) . . . . .   Yes   No

7. Entries are listed by author or title where no author is given (47) . . .   Yes   No

8. I have not included entries unrelated to the topic of my paper (47) . . .   Yes   No

Comments:

_____

_____

_____

_____

Writer's Signature_____

Instructor's Signature_____ Date _____

Checklist for Formal Report or White Paper

Directions: Please fill out the checklist below. Circle yes or no for each item listed. Make any comments necessary in the space provided. Page numbers following each item indicate the reference to the page or pages where you will find information on how to complete the item.

1. I have identified the purpose of the report or paper (65) . . . .   Yes   No

2. I have followed the conventions of formal writing (57–63) . . . .   Yes   No

3. I have provided an introduction (65–66) . . . .   Yes   No

4. I have included citations of source material (65) . . . .   Yes   No

5. I have included background information for the readers (66–67) . . .   Yes   No

6. I have discussed how the issue was dealt with historically and in
   other venues (66) . . . .   Yes   No

7. I have used mostly simple sentences and an economy of
   expression (69) . . . .   Yes   No

8. I have presented conclusions and recommendations (68–69) . . . . . .   Yes   No

9. I have included a reference section (65) . . . .   Yes   No

Comments:

_____

_____

_____

_____

Writer's Signature _____

Instructor's Signature _____   Date _____

Checklist for a Guidebook or Handbook

Directions: Please fill out the checklist below. Circle yes or no for each item listed. Make any comments necessary in the space provided. Page numbers following each item indicate the reference to the page or pages where you will find information on how to complete the item.

1. I have provided an introduction (71) .... Yes   No

2. I have included backup information in appendices (72) .... Yes   No

3. I have explained each step clearly and concisely (71–72) .... Yes   No

4. Each step in the process is presented with economy
   of expression (72) .... Yes   No

5. I have used simple sentences and avoided technical language (73) .. Yes   No

6. I have followed the conventions of formal writing (57–63) .... Yes   No

7. I have included a reference section (72) .... Yes   No

8. I have included a table of contents (72) .... Yes   No

Comments:

_____

_____

_____

_____

Writer's Signature_____

Instructor's Signature_____ Date _____

Checklist for Staff Development Programs

Directions: Please fill out the checklist below. Circle yes or no for each item listed. Make any comments necessary in the space provided. Page numbers following each item indicate the reference to the page or pages where you will find information on how to complete the item.

1. I have developed a needs assessment and included it in an appendix (75) . . . .   Yes   No

2. I have identified expected outcomes of the program (76) . . . .   Yes   No

3. I have identified personnel needs and job descriptions (76) . . . .   Yes   No

4. I have developed an organizational plan for the program (77) . . . . .   Yes   No

5. I have identified workshop presenters and workshop leaders (77) . .   Yes   No

6. I have defined the role of the evaluator (79) . . . .   Yes   No

7. I have included resource needs for the program (78) . . . .   Yes   No

8. I have a plan to meet the differentiated needs of participants (78) . .   Yes   No

9. I have included strategies for involving participants (78) . . . .   Yes   No

10. I have developed an evaluation plan (79) . . . .   Yes   No

Comments:

_____

_____

_____

_____

Writer's Signature_____

Instructor's Signature_____   Date _____

Checklist for Preparing Program Evaluations

Directions: Please fill out the checklist below. Circle yes or no for each item listed. Make any comments necessary in the space provided. Page numbers following each item indicate the reference to the page or pages where you will find information on how to complete the item.

1. I have included background information on the program (82–83) . . Yes No

2. I have included a timeline and schedule of activities (83) . . . . Yes No

3. I have questions for interviews with managers, personnel, and stakeholders (83) . . . . Yes No

4. I have a schedule for observations and noted what needs to be observed (83) . . . . Yes No

5. I have prepared a final report including program strengths and limitations (83–85) . . . . Yes No

6. I have included a narrative of what was learned including recommendations (84–85) . . . . Yes No

7. I have included citations and a reference section in the report (83) . Yes No

8. I have outlined the agenda and process of the final open report (85) . . . . Yes No

9. I have followed the conventions of formal writing (57–63) . . . . Yes No

Comments:

_____

_____

_____

_____

Writer's Signature_____

Instructor's Signature_____ Date _____

Checklist for Grant Proposals

Directions: Please fill out the checklist below. Circle yes or no for each item listed. Make any comments necessary in the space provided. Page numbers following each item indicate the reference to the page or pages where you will find information on how to complete the item.

1. I have followed the guidelines of the RFP (87) .... Yes   No

2. I have specifically identified the problem/issue being
   addressed (87) .... Yes   No

3. I have defined the interventions clearly and concisely (87) .... Yes   No

4. I have developed goals and specific objectives for the
   program (88) .... Yes   No

5. I have provided sequences of activities for goals
   and objectives (87–88) .... Yes   No

6. Benchmarks and expected outcomes have been developed (88) .... Yes   No

7. I have noted the evaluation strategies/protocols to be used (87) .... Yes   No

8. I have prepared a budget with seven categories (88) .... Yes   No

9. I have identified personnel needed for the program (88) .... Yes   No

10. I have identified personnel roles within the program (88) .... Yes   No

11. Stakeholders have been noted including non-program
    personnel (88) .... Yes   No

12. I have addressed compliance issues (88–89) .... Yes   No

13. I have included demographic data (88) .... Yes   No

14. I have followed the conventions of formal writing (57–63) .... Yes   No

Comments:

_____

_____

_____

_____

Writer's Signature_____

Instructor's Signature_____   Date _____

Checklist for Action Research

Directions: Please fill out the checklist below. Circle yes or no for each item listed. Make any comments necessary in the space provided. Page numbers following each item indicate the reference to the page or pages where you will find information on how to complete the item.

1. I have clearly stated the purpose of the action research (91–92) .... Yes   No

2. I have identified specific objectives for the action research (91–92) ... Yes   No

3. I have established a rationale for the action research (92) .... Yes   No

4. I have cited sources and included a reference page (92) .... Yes   No

5. I have defined the intervention or interventions clearly and concisely (92) .... Yes   No

6. The process of implementation has been sequentially presented (93) .... Yes   No

7. I have included a timeline of the components of the interventions (91–92) .... Yes   No

8. I have developed a well-defined evaluation design (93) .... Yes   No

9. I have prepared conclusions and recommendations (94) .... Yes   No

10. I have followed the conventions of formal writing (57–63) .... Yes   No

Comments:

_____

_____

_____

_____

Writer's Signature_____

Instructor's Signature_____ Date _____

Checklist for Personal Response Papers

Directions: Please fill out the checklist below. Check yes or no for each item listed. Make any comments in the space provided. Page numbers following the item refer to the page numbers on which you can find information about how to complete the item.

1. I have included an introduction that is headed by the full
   title (95) . . . . Yes   No

2. I have stated the purpose of the paper in the introduction (95) . . . . . Yes   No

3. The importance of the issue was included in the
   introduction (95) . . . . Yes   No

4. I have included a background and history of the topic
   of issue (95–96) . . . . Yes   No

5. The background/history has level two and three headings
   if needed (96) . . . . Yes   No

6. A discussion sectiion is included (96–97) . . . . Yes   No

7. The discussion section contains a summary (97) . . . . Yes   No

8. An interpretation category is included in the discussion (97) . . . . Yes   No

9. Conclusions are included in the discussion section (98–99) . . . . Yes   No

10. Recommendations are included in the discussion section (98) . . . . . Yes   No

11. I have followed the conventions of formal writing (57–63) . . . . Yes   No

Comments:

_____

_____

_____

_____

Writer's Signature _____

Instructor's Signature _____   Date _____

Checklist for Writing Online

Directions: Please fill out the checklist below. Circle yes or no for each item listed. Make any comments in the space provided. Page numbers following the items refer to pages on which information about the item can be located.

1. My online writing has been clear, concise, and cogent (101) .... Yes   No

2. I have met the expectations of length of assignments and time frame (101) .... Yes   No

3. I have participated in threaded discussions (102) .... Yes   No

4. I have participated in chat sessions (102–103) .... Yes   No

5. I understand the importance of communication and do it regularly (103–104) .... Yes   No

6. I have read evaluations of my assignments and discussions (104–105) .... Yes   No

7. I understand the place of blogs and wikis in online writing (105–106) .... Yes   No

8. I follow the conventions of formal writing in my online writing (57–63) .... Yes   No

Comments:

_____

_____

_____

_____

Writer's Signature _____

Instructor's Signature _____ Date _____

Checklist for Developing Curriculum

Directions: Please fill out the checklist given below. Circle yes or no for each item listed. Make any comments in the space provided. Page numbers following the item are the reference or pages to the pages where you will find information about how to complete the item.

1. I have completed the introduction (107–108) .... Yes   No

2. My lessons are linked together in a unit, theme,
   or area of focus (107) .... Yes   No

3. Identified state (or district) standards are included (108) .... Yes   No

4. Long range outcomes are included for the lesson
   sequence (107–108) .... Yes   No

5. An objective (s) is included for each individual lesson (108–109) ... Yes   No

6. A time frame is included for lesson or lessons (109) .... Yes   No

7. Classroom structures and program materials are included (109–110) .. Yes   No

8. Technology used for each lesson is included (110–111) .... Yes   No

9. Cognitive expectation for each lesson are included (111) .... Yes   No

10. Teaching strategies for each lesson are included (112–113) .... Yes   No

11. SDAIE strategies are listed for each lesson (114–115) .... Yes   No

11. Assessment strategies for each lesson are included (115) .... Yes   No

12. Instructional processes for each lesson are included (116) .... Yes   No

13. A reflection on the lesson is included (116) .... Yes   No

14. I have used APA format and style for narrative sections (57–63) .... Yes   No

15. I have used an supervised approved format for lessons (116–117) ... Yes   No

Comments:

_____

_____

_____

_____

Writer's Signature_____

Instructor's Signature_____ Date _____

Suggested Scoring Rubrics

Below is a suggested scoring rubric for review of literature papers and research papers. Each number represents and "up to" number. You may make any adjustments needed for your class or for your course. The first scoring is for review of literature papers, the second is for research studies. You may use your own scoring rubric. This is just a possible rubric.

Review of Literature Papers

Research Studies

C

Suggested Evaluation Guide

Below are suggested evaluation deductions from papers. You can use this or one of your own construction. Any changes you wish to make can be used for your class. The numbers indicate the suggested loss of points. If the number is two or more you can deduct up to that number.

1. Major syntax error (comma fault, run on, fragment) 3
2. Failure to follow APA format as found in *Handbook* 5
3. More than three agreement errors 1
4. Organization of paper 4
5. Reference errors 1
6. Errors in citations 1
7. Errors in quotations (block quotations, direct quotes, page numbers) 1
8. Errors in tense (consistent use of wrong tense) 3
9. Referent errors 1
10. Spacing errors (everything is double spaced) 2
11. Errors in table of contents (where required) 1
12. Errors in abstract (number of words, not blocked, missing some elements 1
13. Word choice (use precise word) 1
14. Syntax (mostly simple sentences; some compound or complex sentences) 2

15. Use of superscript/subscript except in certain mathematics or
    science formulae 1

16. Errors in ellipses 1

17. Other errors (to be determined by instructor) 2

Format for Presentation of Paper

This format is designed for oral presentations. Power Point presentations can be used in conjunction with oral presentations. Other media may also be used. Organization is key to a strong presentation. As Shakespeare noted "brevity is the soul of wit." Do not be loquacious or verbose. As we have already stated, verbosity is the last refuge of mediocrity. We have keyed this presentation format to a brief presentation of five to eight minutes with two minutes for questions and comments. Longer presentations can go into greater detail and more specificity. They will take more time, but should follow the same format presented below. The presentation format is consistent with the organization of the paper.

Review of Literature Paper

1. State the purpose of your paper.
2. Establish the importance of the topic. This can be done in one or two sentences.
3. Note why you chose this topic.
4. Identify the categories and subcategories of the review of literature.
5. Highlight one or two salient points from each category.
6. In the discussion summarize your review of literature.
7. In the discussion interpret your review of literature.
8. Cite your conclusions.
9. Make your recommendations.

This is all you do for a review of literature paper. For brief presentations, this kind of oral presentation can be done in five minutes or less. Longer presentations, if agreed upon by the instructor or supervisor, can be made.

Research Studies

1. State the purpose of your study. Include information about area of study, limitations, variables, and other pertinent information. State these briefly.
2. Establish the importance of your topic. Use citations as needed.
3. Tell why you selected the topic.
4. Name the categories and subcategories of the review of literature.
5. Identify salient points from the review of literature including other studies about the topic.
6. For the method section restate the purpose of the study, mention time frame, limitations, population, sampling, process, data collection, data analysis, and assessment and evaluation. Do this briefly and avoid any redundancies. Sometimes you can bring two or more categories of the method section together. Tailor the details to the allotted time frame for presentation.
7. Present the results section by noting the variables tested, the and the statistical measures used for analysis.
8. Provide result for each variable keyed to statements on surveys, questionnaires, and interviews.
9. Note the ones on which you are reporting and give results for each.
10. Inferential and correlational statistical analyses require statements of significance.
11. Note any comments from surveys or questionnaires.
12. Establish the meaning of the results in a summative statement.
13. Summarize the review of literature and emphasize how it related to your study.
14. Correlate your findings with the review of literature.
15. Interpret the meaning of your findings including interpretation of the literature reviewed.
16. State your conclusions.
17. State your recommendations.

With careful organization and the presentation of only the most important information, a brief report of this kind can be completed in five to eight minutes with a few minutes for questions and comments following. Any presentation should be tightly organized, succinctly presented, as well as being clear and cogent to the audience. Longer presentations can, of course be allowed by the instructor or supervisor. Best wishes to you on your presentation.

Sample References

Below are listed some references most of which are taken directly from the APA manual. Review these and if you have additional questions, please ask your instructor or supervisor or refer directly to the APA manual.

Book, two authors

Steinaker, N. W., & Bell, M. R. (1979). *The experiential taxonomy: A new approach to teaching and learning.* New York, NY: Academic Press.

Journal article, three to six authors

Saywitz, K. J., Mannarino, A. P., Berliner, L., & Cohen, J. A. (2000). Treatment for Sexually abused children and adolescents. *American Psychologist, 55,* 1040–1049.

Journal article with DOI

Herbts-Damm, K. L., & Kulik, J. A. (2005). Volunteer support, marital status, and the times of terminally ill patients. *Health Psychology, 24,* 225–229. doi: 10.1037/0278-6133.24.2.225.

Magazine article

Kandel, E. R., & Squire, L. R. (2000, November 10), Neuroscience: Breaking down scientific barriers to the study of brain and mind. *Science, 290,* 1112–1120.

Daily newspaper article, no author

New drug appears to sharply cut risk of death from heart failure. (1993, July 15). *The Washington Post*, p. A12.

Abstract as original source

Wood, N. J., Young, S. L., Fanselow, M. S., & Butcher, L. L. (1991). MAP-2 expression in cholinoceptive pyramidal cells or rodent cortex and hippocampus is altered by Pavlovian conditioning [abstract]. *Society for Neuroscience Abstracts.* 17, 480.

Book, third edition, Jr. in name

Mitchell, T. R., & Larson, J. R., Jr. (1987). *People in organizations: An introduction to organizational behavior* (3rd ed.). New York: McGraw-Hill.

Edited book

Gibbs, J. T., & Huang, L. N. (Eds.), (1991). *Children of color: Psychological Interventions with minority youth.* San Francisco, CA: Jossey-Bass.

Article or chapter from an edited book, two editors

Bjork, R. A. (1989). Retrieval inhibition as an adaptive mechanism in human memory. In H. L. Roediger II & F. I. M. Craik (Eds.), *Varieties of memory & consciousness* (pp. 309–330). Hillsdale, NJ: Erlbaum.

Entry in an encyclopedia

Bergmann, P. G. (1993). Relativity. In *The new encyclopaedia Britannica* (Vol. 26, pp. 5 501–558). Chicago: Encyclopedia Britannica.

Note: When the article has no author listed, place the title in the author position.

Report available from ERIC

Mead, J. V. (1992). *Looking at old photographs: Investigating the teacher tales that no novice teachers bring with them* (Report No. NCRTL-RR-9204). East Lansing, MI: National Center for Research on Teacher Learning. (ERIC Document Reproduction Service No. ED346082).

Published proceedings of meetings or symposia

Deci, E. L., & Ryan, R. M. (1991). A motivational approach to self: Integration in pers personality. In R. Dienstbier (Ed.). *Nebraska Symposium on Motivation: Vol. 38. Perspectives on motivation* (pp. 237–288). Lincoln: University of Nebraska Press.

Doctoral dissertations and master's theses abstracted in Dissertation Abstracts International from the University of Michigan

Brower, D. L. (1993). Employee assistant programs supervisory referrals: Characteristics of referring and nonreferring supervisors. *Dissertation Abstracts International 54* (01) 534B. (UMI No. 9315947)

Unpublished manuscript not submitted for publication

Stinson, C., Milbrath, C, Reidbord, S. & Bucci, W. (1992). *Thematic segmentation of psychotherapy transcripts for convergent analyses.* Unpublished manuscript.

Manuscript in progress or submitted for publication but not yet accepted

Steinaker, N. W., Mbuva, J, & Holm, M. (2005). *A taxonomy of motivation: From theory to practice.* Manuscript submitted for publication.

Internet articles based on a print source

VandenBos, G., Knapp, S., & Doe, J. (2001). Role of reference elements in the section of resources by psychology undergraduates [Electronic version], *Journal of Bibliographic Research*, 5, 117–123.

Stand-alone internet document, no author identified, no date

GVU's 8th WWW user survey. (n.d.). Retrieved August 8, 2000, from http://www.cc.gatech.edu/gvu/user_surveys/survey-1997-10/

Message posted to a newsgroup

Chalmers, D. (2000, November 17). Seeing with sound [Msg 1]. Message posted to news://sci.psychology.consciousness

Electronic copy of a journal article, retrieved from database

Borman, W. C., Hanson, M. A., Oppler, S. H., Pulakos, E. D., & White, L. A. (1993). Roles of early supervisor performance. *Journal of Applied Psychology*, 78, 443–449.

Preparing Surveys and Questionnaires

Often in preparation for a research study you need to prepare a survey or a questionnaire.Both need to begin with a strong focus on the purpose of your study. Develop a simple and direct set of directions for filling out the survey or questionnaire. Start your survey or questionnaire with demographic questions about the population you are asking to respond to your survey or your questionnaire. Demographic information includes such elements as age, gender, work assignment, ethnicity, area of residence, and other descriptive demographic information. Demographic information is important because from this information you may identify some or all of the variables you wish to test.

Next you develop statements or questions to gather responses from your population. Determine the most important information you want to obtain and include those statements or questions early in the survey or questionnaire. Make statements or ask questions that are clearly written and can be easily understood by your population. Avoid value words wherever possible and avoid words that can be interpreted in more than one way. Make your statements and questions specific, to the point, and limited to identified information you wish to obtain. Make sure that each question or statement addresses only one issue or area about which to respond. In a survey make space available to comments by respondents. If you wish to have them respond to a specific statement, make space available after that statement. You may also make space available at the end of the survey. In a questionnaire establish some limits to your questions. You may want to ask your respondents to use only the space provided. You may also want to get as much information as possible, so invite them to extend their responses if they wish.

If you are using a survey, you may use a Likert Scale which has strongly agree, agree, disagree, strongly disagree possible responses. You may use a numeric scale and ask your population to circle the number that describes their response. Make sure you identify what each number means. You may also use a semantic differential scale if you wish. There are a variety of formats for your survey. Select the one that best fits the population you are studying.

You may also use any of these formats for a questionnaire if you wish. Many questionnaires are set up so that respondents can make comments. In a survey or questionnaire you can tally your responses and then use statistical measures to analyze, assess, and interpret data from the survey or questionnaire. You can summarize or categorize the comments. You may also wish to identify the responses anonymously through the demographic data you have collected. Make sure as you develop your instrument that it can serve to elicit responses that will help you gather the data you need to find results that focus on the major purpose of your study.

Elements of Formal Grammar Usage

It is very important that you become familiar with the grammatical expectations for formal writing and use them consistently. We have discussed many of these expectations in the writing tips which follow each section. A number of these expectations are also found in the common errors section and in the section on conventions of formal writing. We felt however, there was a need to bring together information about grammar in a section of this work where it would be easily accessible to you, the writer. While we have included many grammatical expectations, there are others about which you need to be aware. The content of this appendix is designed as a quick reference to help you clarify identified grammar issues related to formal writing. It is not as a complete guide to grammar. You should have available a more complete guide when you are writing. There are many resources you can use. Among them Turabian (2007), Strunk and White (2000), and the *Manual* of the APA. This section on grammar is divided into three categories: Punctuation, syntax, and other grammar expectations. This information is organized alphabetically by category for easy use. Refer to it as needed when you are preparing your papers.

Punctuation

Abbreviations: Abbreviations are seldom used in formal writing. Generally the whole word is written and abbreviations are not used. Some forms of address such as Mr., Mrs., Ms, and Dr. may be used. Abbreviations like Sr., Jr, III, and IV (senior, junior, third, and fourth) may be included in a formal paper. Certain abbreviations for scholarly degrees and titles of respect following full names are set off by two commas when used in text. State names can be given their two letter code abbreviations. You may abbreviate such terms as avenue, boulevard, street, and directions (N, S, E, W). Abbreviations are followed by a period.

Active voice: The active voice is more direct than the passive voice. The active voice in writing is more concise and more definite.

> Active voice: *I will always remember my first visit to Denver.*

> Passive voice: *My first visit to Denver will always be remembered by me.*

Acronyms: A series of letters or a word formed from the initial letter of each of the successive parts of a compound term. For example: *Heuristic Electronic Lesson Planner* (HELP). Note that after the first use of the compound term, the acronym is used in parentheses. In successive usages the acronym may be used in place of the compound term without parentheses. In the first use of an acronym, the term must be written out in words.

Anthropomorphism: Attributing human characteristics to animals or inanimate sources. For example: *Research said. The school program was persuaded.* A writer should start the sentence with the subject. This will eliminate most anthropomorphisms.

Brackets: Brackets [ ] are primarily used for insertions into quoted matter for editorial comments, corrections, and clarifications inserted into quoted matter.

Capitalization: A capital letter is used in the first letter of proper nouns (names of persons, places, and specific things). Proper nouns that have lost their original meaning and have become part of general language use are not capitalized. An example is roman numerals. The first letter of the first word of a sentence is capitalized. In titles of books and articles in reference lists, capitalize only the first word. Also capitalize the first word after a colon or dash. Capitalize trade and brand names of drugs, equipment, and foods.

Colons: The colon is used to introduce a clause or a phrase that expands, clarifies, or exemplifies the meaning of what precedes it. In formal writing the first word following a colon is capitalized. A colon is used between chapter and verse in referring to scripture.

Commas: Commas are used more frequently in formal writing than in other writing styles. Commas are used to separate a series of three or more items in a list. They are used after yes and no. They are used between appositives, following an adverbial beginning of a sentence, and following author's names in a reference section. Enclose parenthetic expression in sentences with commas. Commas follow abbreviations of academic degrees and titles. Place a comma before a conjunction introducing an independent clause. A comma follows words such as *namely, that is, nevertheless,* and *for example.* When a long prepositional phrase introduces a sentence, it is followed by a comma. A comma is used to separate main clauses joined by a coordinating conjunction such as *and, but, or, nor,* or *so.* A comma is used with compound predicates. Commas are used to set off transitional words or phrases such as *indeed.*

Dashes: Dashes are seldom used in formal writing. In a few instances a dash can be used to introduce an element that emphasizes or explains the main clause through of one or more key words.

Hyphens: When two or more words are combined to form a compound adjective, a hyphen can be used. Do not begin a line or end a line with a hyphen. Prefixes such as *mid, multi,* and *non* do not require hyphens.

Italics: You use italics for for titles of books, periodicals, and microfilm publications, italicize letters that are used as test scores or scales: A *t* test or the *n* was thirty.

Parentheses: Parentheses are principally used in the text to set off parenthetical elements and to enclose the source of a quotation or a paraphrase. A citation is enclosed by parentheses.

Passive voice: A verb form indicating that the subject is being acted on. The passive voice is acceptable in expository writing, but is less used in formal writing.

Periods: A period ends a sentence or a sentence that is neither a question nor an exclamation. A period is used after abbreviations. Periods are used with a person's initials followed by a space. A period follows numerals and letters in an outline.

Quotation Marks: Quotation marks enclose direct quotations but not indirect quotations or paraphrases. Quotation marks enclose fragments of quoted material. Quotation marks are not included in blocked quotes of more than forty words.

Semicolons: A semicolon should be used between the parts of a compound sentence of two or more independent clauses when not connected by a conjunction. If clauses of a compound sentence are long and have commas within them, they should be separated by a semicolon. If the second clause is preceded by an adverb such as *accordingly, besides, then, therefore,* or *thus,* and not by a conjunction, the semicolon is required.

Titles of tests: Titles of tests are capitalized except for articles and prepositions. Do not capitalize the generic titles of test such as a *normative test* or a *standardized test.* Do not capitalize words such as *test* or *scale* if they refer to subscales of tests.

 # Syntax

Abruptness: A series of short sentences can cause choppiness or abruptness in sentences. Varied sentence lengths are more appropriate. Direct declarative sentences in the active voice with simple, common words are usually best. Read your paper aloud to ensure that there is no abruptness in the flow of ideas and the smoothness of expression.

Clauses: A group of words containing a subject and predicate and functioning as a part of a compound or complex sentences. A semicolon is used to separate independent clauses without a coordinating convention.

Comma fault: The use of a comma instead of a semicolon to link two independent clauses. This is a major syntax error. It is sometimes called a comma splice.

Compound sentences: Two or more independent clauses joined by a coordinating conjunction, or a semicolon.

Economy of expression: Say only what needs to be said. Avoid noun strings. Eliminate redundancy, overuse of the passive voice, and detailed descriptions. Do not use clumsy prose. Do not elaborate or embellish. Short words and short sentences are easier to understand than are long ones.

Jargon: Jargon is the continuous use of technical vocabulary even in places where it is relevant. Jargon is also the substituting of a euphemistic phrase for a familiar term. *Momentarily felt scarcity* for *poverty*, and you should scrupulously avoid such jargon.

Orderly presentation of ideas: Thought units must be presented in an orderly manner. In this way readers will understand what you are presenting. To do this you must aim for continuity in words, concepts, and thematic development throughout your paper. Continuity can be achieved through punctuation. They cue the reader to pauses, inflections, subordination, and pacing normally heard in speaking.

Precision and clarity: Say only what is needed. If you are frugal with words you will write a more readable manuscript. You can tighten long papers by eliminating redundancy, wordiness, jargon, evasiveness, overuse of passive voice, and clumsy prose. Eliminate overly detailed descriptions, gratuitous embellishments, elaboration of the obvious, and irrelevant observations or asides.

Redundancy: Writers can become redundant in an effort to be emphatic. Use no more words than are necessary to convey meaning. Do not embellish or repeat for emphasis.

Run on sentences: Compound sentences in which independent clauses are not separated by punctuation or a connecting conjunction. This is a major syntax error.

Sentence fragment: A group of words that is not a complete sentence, but is punctuated as one. *If it mattered greatly.* This is a major syntax error.

Sentence length: While most of your writing will be in short simple sentences, you must avoid abruptness or choppiness. Varied sentence length helps maintain interest and comprehension. Direct, declarative sentences with simple common words are usually best.

Simple sentence: A short direct, declarative sentence with a subject-verb or a subject-verb-objective configuration. Use clear, concise, and cogent simple sentences throughout most of your paper.

Wordiness: Unconstrained wordiness lapses into embellishment and flowery writing and are inappropriate in formal writing. Wordiness can impede the ready grasp of ideas.

Other Grammar Issues

Adjective: A word or words that describe a noun.

Adverb: A word or words that modifies a verb, adjective, adverb preposition phrase, clause, or sentence.

Agreement: A grammatical relationship that involves the correspondence in number either between subject and verb in a sentence or between a pronoun and its antecedent.

Case: The form of a noun or pronoun that reflects it grammatical function in a sentence as subject (they), object (them), or possessor (their). For example: *She* gave *her* employees a raise that pleased *them* greatly.

Colloquialism: A word or expression appropriate to informal conversation but not usually suitable for formal writing. Colloquialisms diffuse meaning.

Comparisons: Ambiguous or illogical comparison result from omission of key verbs or from nonparallel structure. An illogical comparison occurs when parallelism is overlooked for the sake of brevity. *Her salary was lower than a convenience store clerk* instead of *Her salary was lower than that of a convenience store clerk.*

He/she: Avoid the overuse of he/she when referring to one person where gender is not known. In most cases the sentence can be rewritten to avoid the he/she.

Noun: A word that names a person, place, thing or idea.

Preposition: A word that relates its object to another word in the sentence.

Pronoun: Any of a small group of words that are used for substitutes for nouns, phrases, or clauses and refer to someone or something named or understood in context.

Proper noun: The name of a particular person, place, or thing. Proper nouns are capitalized. Common nouns name classes of people, places, and things and are not capitalized.

Tense: The time of a verb's action or state of being, such as past, present, or future. *Saw, see, will see.* In formal writing past tense and present perfect tenses (has been) are used throughout the paper except in the interpretation category of the discussion section. Conclusionsand recommendations can be written in past tense, present tense, or in future tense. Tense errors are very common in formal writing and should be carefully avoided.

Unbiased language: When referring to a person or persons choose words that are accurate, clear, and free from bias. For example using *man* to refer to all human beings is not as acceptable the phrase *men and women*. *Gender* is the term to use when referring to men and women as social groups. Writing without bias is recognizing that differences should be mentioned only when relevant.

Verb: a word or group of words that expresses the action or indicates the state of being of the subject. Verbs activate sentences.

Writing Tips

It is important that you follow these grammatical expectations in terms of punctuation, syntax, and other issues of grammar. Whenever you have concerns about the structure of sentences, the correct or appropriate punctuation to use, how to ensure the orderly flow of information, and to ensure economy of expression you should refer to this section of the *Handbook* and to the writing tips following each of the sections of the *Handbook*. It is your obligation as a writer of formal papers to learn these grammatical expectations and to use them effectively in your paper. We have suggested other sources that are more complete and suggest that you use at least one for additional grammar specifics and information.

In this glossary of terms are entries, many of which you will use in your review of literature or in your research study. Others are included that you may need as you review literature and other studies related to your paper or research study.

A

Action research. Research done by a practitioner in single case studies or small group interventions.

Analysis of covariance (ANCOVA). A procedure for determining whether the difference between the mean scores of two or more groups on one or more dependent variables is statistically significant.

Analytic induction. In qualitative research, the process of inferring themes and patterns from an examination of data.

Analytic reporting. In a qualitative research report, the use of an objective writing style where the researchers voice is silent or subdued and other conventions typical to quantitative research.

Anecdotal record. A record of behaviors or activities that occur at designated times or when the behaviors or activities occur.

Aptitude test. A measure of abilities that are assumed to be relevant to performance on an identified type of skill or area of achievement.

Artifacts. Objects created by members of past or present cultures.

Axiology. The study of the nature, types, and criteria of values, and value judgments especially in ethics.

B

Baseline. In single case studies the natural behavior patterns of the subject of the study.

Bias. Personal and unreasonable distortion of judgment in such a way that certain facts are habitually overlooked, distorted, or falsified.

C

Case study research. Study of a phenomenon in its natural context from the perspective of the participants.

Category. In the review of literature a major component of the review. Categories are now introduced by level two headings. There must be at least two in the review of literature. A category is a component of frequency count data.

Chain of evidence. In qualitative research the validation of the study's findings by clear meaningful links in terms of the study's questions, the raw data analysis and findings.

Chi square. An inferential test of statistical significance used when research data are in the form of frequency counts in two or more categories.

Citation. Information about a document or resource that one would need in order to locate it. A citation contains the name of the author and the year of publication. It is in parantheses following the quotation or paraphrase. If no author is listed use the first two words of the title.

Cognitive taxonomy. A classification of cognition developed by Bloom and colleagues. Initially the taxonomy had six categories. This was revised to seven including: Memory, translation, interpretation, application, analysis, synthesis, and evaluation.

Cohort longitudinal research. An investigation in which changes in a population over time are studied by selecting a different sample at each data collection point from a population that remains constant.

Correlational research. An investigation that seeks to discover the direction and magnitude of the relationships between two or more variables through the use of correlational statistics.

Curriculum: What is to be taught to prepare students for a given purpose. Curriculum has structure and sequence. It contains content areas that are interrelated and interdependent.

D

Dependent variable. The variable the researcher is interested in measuring to determine how it is different for groups with different experience or characteristics.

Descriptor. A term or used to classify information about the topic in the classification of documents or to describe briefly categories of information.

Descriptive statistics. Statistical analyses which describe the data collected. They include mean, median, mode, range, and standard deviation. In qualitative research, investigation that involves providing a detailed portrayal of one or more cases.

Diagnostic test. A test used to determine a student's strengths and weaknesses in a particular subject.

Disaggregated data. Data reported in the results section on identified groups within the population tested.

E

Educational Resources Information Center (ERIC). A federally funded agency that provides information resources to the education community.

Emergent design. In qualitative studies, the practice of changing the design of the study or evaluation as the evaluator or researcher gains new insights into the concerns and issues of the group being studied.

Emic perspective. Research participants perceptions of their social reality.

Epistemology. The study of the nature of knowledge.

Experiential taxonomy. A *gestalt* taxonomy developed by Steinaker & Bell that incorporates the cognitive and affective taxonomies in a five step sequence that can be used for teaching and evaluating student work.

Ethnography. The in depth study of life in an identified culture and patterns within it. The focus is on society and culture. Ethnographic studies uncover and describe beliefs, values, and attitudes of a group.

Etic perspective. The researcher's perspective of the research participants social reality.

Experimenter bias. A situation in which the experimenter or author's expectations about what will occur are transmitted to the research participants behavior in the study is affected. Also a situation in which the researcher's expectations affect data collection and data analysis.

Extinction. The practice of behavior modification through the withdrawal of an intervention in behavioral research.

F

Formative evaluation. Evaluation of the process of a study done while the program is underway.

G

Generalizability. Researcher's ability to generalize results from the sample from which it was drawn and relate those generalizations to transferability.

Grounded theory. An approach to theory development in qualitative research. Grounded theory emerges from the data collected and the narrative associated with those data. It is an emergent theory and does not depend on an existing theory.

H

Hermeneutics. A field of inquiry that seeks to understand how individuals develop interpretations and consensus about issues and tasks.

Historical research. A study of past phenomena for the purpose of gaining a better understanding of present institutions, practices, trends, and issues.

Hypothesis. A researcher's prediction, derived from theory or from speculation, about how two or more variables will be related to each other.

I

Independent variable. The treatment or intervention the researcher uses with the experimental group in an experimental design within quantitative research.

Inferential statistics. Statistical protocols designed to determine significance.

Institutional review board (IRB). A committee established by an institution to ensure that participants in research projects will be protected from harm. The IRB reviews and approves research done by members of the institution.

Interrater reliability. A measure to determine if two or more raters reliably measure criteria with similar standards and results.

Interval recording. The recording of observational behaviors at given time intervals.

Item analysis. A set of procedures for determining the difficulty, the reliability, and the validity of each item on a test.

Iteration. A repeated procedure intended to bring to participants in a study or students to a predetermined level of competence.

L

Likert scale. A measure that asks individuals to check their level of agreement with various statements.

Longitudinal research. An investigation that involves describing changes in a sample's characteristics over a specified period of time.

M

Matrix. In a qualitative research report, a type of table that has defined rows and columns for reporting the results of data analyses and other information.

Mean. A measure of central tendency calculated by the sum of the score in a set by the numbers of scores.

Median. A measure of central tendency corresponding to the middle score in a range of scores.

Meta analysis. Statistical procedures to identify trends from the results of a set of studies on the same problem or issue.

Mode. A measure of central tendency corresponding to the most frequently occurring score in a distribution of scores.

Monograph. A professional treatise on a narrow area of learning.

Multiple regression. A statistical procedure for determining the relationship between a criterion variable and a combination of two or more predictor variables.

N

NCE score or normal curve equivalent. A type of scoring with a mean of 50. The scores are continuous and have an equality of units. There are 100 scores in all and they correspond to individual percentages.

Normal curve. A distribution of scores that form a symmetrical, bell shaped curve when plotted on a graph.

O

Objectivity. The extent to which the narrative or the scores on a test by the biases of the researcher or the writer.

Ontology. A branch of metaphysics concerned with the nature and relations of being, the kinds of existents or having being.

Ordinal scale. A measure in which numbers represent a rank ordering of individuals or objects on some variable.

Outlier. A research participant's score on a measure which differs markedly from other scores.

P

Parameter. The boundary of a study, a series of scores, or the characteristics of a population's scores.

Paraphragiarism. Borrowing of another author's writing to such an extent as to constitute the representation of the other author's work as your own. Similar to plagiarism.

Pattern. In qualitative research instances in which certain behaviors, attitudes, or actions are systematically related to each other.

Pearson r. In correlational statistical analysis a mathematical expression of the direction and magnitude of the relationship between two measures with continuous scores.

Percentile. A type of rank score that represents a raw score as the percentage of individuals in the norming group whose scores fall below that score.

Personal communication. An interview with a peer or other person which is cited or quoted in the text of a paper.

Pilot study. A small scale preliminary investigation conducted to develop and test the measures used in a research study.

Positivism. An epistemological belief that reality is independent of those who observe it, and that observations of this reality, if unbiased, constitute scientific knowledge.

Postmodernism. A broad social and philosophical movement that questions the rationality of human action, the use of positivist epistemology, and any human endeavor that claims a privileged position with respect to the search for truth.

Posttest. A measure that is administered following an experimental or control treatment in order to determine the effects of the intervention. A posttest only is a test given to both experimental and control groups following the intervention with the experimental group.

Presentism. Interpreting past events in terms of concepts and perspectives that originated in recent times.

Pretest. A measure administered prior to an experimental treatment or other intervention.

Q

Qualitative research. Inquiry that is grounded in the assumption that individuals construct social reality in the form of meaning and interpretations, and that these constructions tend to be transitory and situational.

Quantitative research. Inquiry that is grounded in the assumption that features of the social environment constitute and objective reality that is relatively constant across time and settings.

R

Random assignment. The process of assigning individuals or groups to the experimental or control treatment in order that each individual or group has an equal chance of being in each group.

Range. The difference between the highest and the lowest scores in a distribution.

Reliability. The extent to which a test yields the same or similar results in repeated administration.

Rubric. A scale to measure different levels of proficiency demonstrated by students.

S

Sampling. The process of selecting members of a research sample from a defined population.

Semantic differential scale. A measure that asks individuals to rate an attitude on a series of bipolar adjective (fair-unfair, valuable-worthless, hot-cold).

Semiotics. The study of sign systems. In particular the study of how objects come to meaning and how sign systems affect human behavior.

Snowball sampling. Cases that are selected by asking one person to recommend others with similar experiences.

Stakeholder. Participants in a study who have an interest in the quality and outcomes of a program. Can be program employees, parents, citizens, or students.

Standard deviation. A measure of the extent that scores in a distribution deviate from their mean.

Statistic. Any number that describes a characteristic of a sample's score on a measure.

Survey research. The use of questionnaires or interviews to collect data about the characteristics, experiences, knowledge, or, opinions of a sample or a population.

T

t Score. A probability distribution used to determine level of statistical significance of an obtained *t* value of the difference between two sample means.

Test. A structured performance situation that can be analyzed to yield numerical scores.

Theory. An explanation of the commonalities and the relationships among observed phenomena in terms of causal structure and processes that are presumed to underlie them.

Triangulation. The use of multiple data collection methods, data sources, analysts, or theories a corroborative evidence for the validity of qualitative research findings.

V

Validity. Measures that determine if the test or measure for data collection is consistent with the content of what is being tested.

Variable. A characteristic of the sample of the population. Data from the characteristic are collected, analyzed and reported.

This paper is designed to provide you with a model of what your formal paper should look like. It is a review of literature paper, not a research paper. In a research paper you would includ the method section and the results section. Most of what we have presented earlier about formal papers has been included in this review of literature. You have the model of the title page and the abstract. Elements of the introduction follow the material we have presented earlier in this work. You can see how the review of literature has been organized. The introductory paragraph, the categories and subcategories follow the format we have suggested. You can read and see how to do your discussion section including summary, interpretation, conclusions, and recommendations.

There are many models for references. You can use the reference included in this paper as well as the model refeences in Appendix E to learn how to prepare references for your own paper. As you prepare your own formal paper you can use this paper to identify format, sequence, categories, and subcategories. Note the sentence structure and the flow of ideas in the paper. Understanding syntax, structure, and sequence of the paper can be valuable to you as you write your own paper. Use this paper along with the materials in the body of this work to help you prepare the best possible formal paper you can. Please note that the page numbers are not sequential with this work, rather, they follow the page sequence of the model paper.

Running head: STANDARDS AND CREATIVE PLANNING

Standards and Creative Planning

Norman W. Terry

National University

Abstract

The purpose of this paper was to review literature on standards, creative planning, and teaching. The use of standards implied performance based instruction with demonstrated outcomes. It was shown that how one teaches was more important to learning than what was taught. Standards have been written to define what was to be taught. They have also been open for utilization of creative methodology. Teachers who planned carefully and used standards to create learning experiences could provide interactive learning at high cognitive levels. It was concluded that creative teaching augmented student learning. It was also concluded that all lessons must reach at least the application level of cognition. It was recommended that teachers receive professional development on creative implementation of standards.

Standards and Creative Planning

The purpose of this paper was to review literature about standards and how planning standards-based instruction could be related to creative and effective teaching. Standards, for the purpose of this paper, were defined as state standards used by states as the expectations for student achievement and demonstrated performance (California State, n. d.).

This topic has been a major area of focus for educators in all states. Darling-Hammond (2001) noted that standards "have become a major policy vehicle" (p. 211). It was further noted that state standards should "be designed as a shell within which the kernel of professional judgment and decision making can function comfortably" (Shulman, 1983, p. 501). Learning should, with careful planning, be an experience the student could internalize (Steinaker & Bell, 1979). Reeves (2004) observed that every lesson and daily activity should relate to an identified standard. In order to implement a standards driven instructional program, teachers should "identify the best practices in standards-based teaching and learning" (Reeves, 2004, p. 53).

Every lesson or activity should achieve at least the application level of cognition. A linked series of lessons should develop student learning at the analysis, synthesis, and evaluation levels of cognition (Steinaker, 2006b).

When teachers have planned lessons based on standards, the "how of teaching becomes more important than what we teach" (Steinaker, 2007b, p. 4). This meant that teachers must focus on experiential learning and helping students internalize what they have been exposed to, participated with, identified as important, and internalized. Furthermore, they needed to be able to disseminate what they have learned (Steinaker & Bell, 1979). Standards, in this context have become performance goals, which allowed the teacher to plan carefully and to include creativity as a major dimension of instruction. Thus, the teacher and the student could work together creatively and interactively to achieve the performance standard. Creativity became a sequential and integral part of the context of learning and provided the students with the ability to demonstrate the performance implicit within the standard (Steinaker, 2006b). Steinaker (2007b) further stated that the use of standards provided a basis and incentive for creative and experiential learning. It was concluded by Reeves (2004) that "teachers who create effective standards-based performance assignments are the real heroes of the standards movement" (p. 140).

I chose this topic because I wanted to investigate standards-based education as it related to creative planning and to the instructional process. I have believed that the more informed I became about implementing a creative instructional program, the more effective I could become as a teacher.

STANDARDS AND CREATIVE PLANNING   5

Review of Literature

The review of literature was organized with three headings. These headings were state standards, lesson planning with standards, and creativity and standards. The heading on lesson planning had two subheadings. These subheadings were standards-based planning and heuristic electronic lesson planner.

State Standards

Every state has developed standards or performance descriptors (Reeves, 2004). Each state has its unique structure and organization. Some states provide standards and performance outcomes and little else. Other states detail support materials, references, suggested teaching strategies and examples (Education World, 2006). Each state has developed a specific format for its standards or performance outcomes. Teachers in Idaho, for example, were provided with grade level standards K-12 in all content areas along with identified goals and objectives for each grade level. They further provide standard assessments by grade level, information on professional development, and curriculum materials (Education World, 2006). Iowa was the only state not having standards. Instead, they have performance level descriptors (Education World, 2006). Each state department of education provided some support information for teachers to help them in working with students for achieving the standards (Education World,

2006). In almost every state, there were many standards in all content areas and at all grade levels (Education World, 2006). Darling-Hammond (2001) saw standards as a means to reform or transform schools. She conceptualized standards as a means of transforming teaching and involving students in the process of learning. She expressed concern about the number of standards and the expectation that the teachers need to cover each standard. She further felt there needed to be fewer standards and more in depth learning (Darling-Hammond, 2001). Shulman (1983) described standards as being "designed as a shell within which the kernel of professional judgment and decision making can function comfortably" (p. 501).

The use of standards or generic objectives has not been a new phenomenon in American education.

Franklin Bobbitt, in 1924, organized a course of study for the elementary grades. He outlined more than 800 objectives and related activities to coincide with predetermined student needs. These activities ranges from "the ability to care for [one's] teeth. . .eyes. . .nose. . .and throat;. . .to keep home appliances in good working condition;. . .spelling and grammar." Bobbitt's methods were quite sophisticated for his day. (as cited in Ornstein & Hunkins, 2004, p. 3)

STANDARDS AND CREATIVE PLANNING   7

The issue of standards has been a part of the American educational

scene since the late seventies. Debates have been continuing. Ornstein and

Hunkins reported:

> As the world becomes increasingly complex, standards appropriate in
>
> simpler times are no longer adequate. In an information age, students
>
> [must] meet higher demands on their levels of knowledge and skills
>
> than did their counterparts in a pre industrial nation. (2004, p. 393)

Based on this premise states have responded with the development of

standards for teachers to use as performance evidence for student

achievement (Steinaker, 2006b). Models of teaching could be related to

standards. Joyce, Weil, with Calhoun (2004) linked each model of teaching

they identified with student achievement and student performance.

There have been issues in state support for standards-based

instruction. A critical issue according to authors at the North Central

Regional Educational Laboratory (NCREL) was resources to support higher

student achievement. NCREL found:

> creating standard-based schools that are accountable for helping all
>
> students reach higher levels of achievement requires schools and districts
>
> to rethink their educational resources—especially time, staffing, and
>
> money. As districts begin to support schools in becoming increasingly
>
> accountable for results, they are finding that schools need: more time for

students in academic subjects and more individualized attention; time and dollars for ongoing teacher professional development and planning; and investment funding for the purchase, introduction, and classroom implementation of new curriculum materials and teaching practices aimed at higher standards. (NCREL, 2006, p. 1)

This was but one issues. There have been many other issues. For example, how to teach to standards has been another. In this area, state departments of education have provided differentiated kinds of support (Education World, 2006). Steinaker (2007b) suggested that professional development be provided for teachers to creatively plan how to teach to the standards in an interactive and creative environment. State personnel have defined performance standards (Education World, 2006). Corollary to student achievement of the performance expected within the standard was the need for "more autonomy and authority in the use of time, the selection and use of staff, and the alignment of funds (NCREL, 2006, p. 1). Further, it has been confirmed that if students had more time focused on academics they could learn more (Prisoners of, 1994). There were other issues and there have been personnel in all states addressing them (Education World, 2006).

Lesson Planning With Standards

Critical to successful student learning has been careful and creative planning. Steinaker and Harrison (1976) noted that "a carefully structured

STANDARDS AND CREATIVE PLANNING   9

instructional program contribute[s] to student [learning]. . . .The

importance of a structured curriculum and instructional program emerges

as the most important factor, in determining whether a student does

achieve as expected (pp. 75-76).

Standards-based planning. Lesson planning focused on achieving

performance-based standards is essential (Steinaker, 2006b). There are

many theoretical perspectives on how students learn (Ornstein & Hunkins,

2004). Bruner (1961) felt that learning involved organizing meaningful

experiences which could be transferred more readily than rote learning.

Dewey (1910) identified this dimension of learning as reflective thinking.

In a standards-based instructional environment, there has been a need for

teachers to carefully plan and sequence a variety of teaching strategies for

all students to learn experientially and interactively (Steinaker & Bell,

1979). Serdyukov (2004) stated, "lesson planning is essential in. . .any

aspect of daily classroom life" (p. 5). Furthermore, "it has become

important that the relationship between the skills and concepts to be

learned be clearly related to and drawn from specific standards. The

achievement standards needed to be kept personal and cooperative, not

competitive" (Steinaker & Leavitt, 2010). Reeves (2004) reported,

"academic standards make it clear that students cannot be complacent

about 'beating' a competitor; they must persist, work, and learn until they

meet the standard" (p. 27). Planning should be based on the achievement

STANDARDS AND CREATIVE PLANNING   10

of standards. This is the imperative of the state education standards and

performance level descriptors (Education World, 2006).

Heuristic electronic lesson planner. One program for teaching

planning keyed to the standards and other professional expectations was the

Heuristic Electronic Lesson Planner (HELP) developed by Steinaker (2007a).

Teachers who have used the program log in, identify the state for which

they wanted standards, selected the grade level, and the content area.

When this was completed, the standards for that content area and grade

level were shown on the screen and the teacher selected the standard on

which the students were to work. The teacher then entered the lesson

objective in the space provided. Time and date of the lesson were

determined by the teacher. Teachers could, on a popup menu, choose the

primary classroom structure used and the technology pertinent to the

lesson. These were on popup menus (Steinaker, 2007a). From a list of

twenty-five sequenced teaching strategies, the teacher chose the ones to be

used. These strategies were keyed to the cognitive taxonomy and when the

strategy deepest into the list of strategies was chosen, the level of cognition

for that lesson was shown in the space for cognition on the program.

Likewise, the teacher chose strategies for specially designed activities in

English (SDAIE). In addition, the teacher selected assessment strategies

from a popup menu. Finally, in a space provided, the teacher wrote each of

the sequential steps in the lesson. After the lesson was completed, in the

STANDARDS AND CREATIVE PLANNING   11

same space, the teacher could write the results of the lesson. The lesson could then be printed. In this way, the teacher had a running record of each standard taught, of each teaching strategy and SDAIE strategy used, the sequence of the lesson, and the outcome of the lesson (Steinaker, 2007a).

In addition to the format described above, there was documentation and information about each of the categories noted (Steinaker, 2007a). This was available to the teacher by clicking on a help button linked to the category. Information about that category was immediately available to the teacher. Professional support for the teacher was provided about the cognitive taxonomy, teaching strategies, classroom structures, SDAIE strategies, types of group structures, assessments, technologies, and classroom instructional organizations (Steinaker, 2007a). This was the only known program that had professional documentation built into it. Teachers who have used the program like it. On said that the program was "really terrific" (Personal communication B. Holzner, November 9, 2006). Building lessons around standards has become for them a natural, effective, and creative planning modality (Steinaker, 2006). As Serdyukov (2004) indicated, "effective lesson planning helps you stay focused" (p. 20). Effective lesson planning through HELP provided a professional and creative format for lesson planning (Steinaker, 2007a).

Creativity and Standards

The how of teaching, as noted by Steinaker (2006b) was more important than the what of teaching. State standards identify the what of teaching (Educational World, 2006). The how of teaching is directly related to creativity. Steinaker and Bell (1979) defined creativity as having five levels. They were "motivation to develop a product, visualization of the product, experimenting with ways to complete the product, actually completing the product, and finally admiring it, showing it, and sharing it" (p. 90). They further identified creativity as "a personal interaction with an idea, with material, or a problem. It is a process that requires sequences and activity unique to the individual and that results in a product, and acquires skill, or a modified behavior" (p. 91).

This definition of creativity along with HELP (Steinaker, 2007a) has provided for teachers a methodology for creating interactive learning experiences for students. Brown and Palinscar (1989) defined this kind of interactive learning and reciprocal teaching. Joyce et al. (2004) defined reciprocal teaching as intrinsic to scaffolding, which could help students "acquire increasing metacognitive control" (p. 15). As teachers involved in creative and reciprocal learning experiences, "they know how to take the initiative in planning. . .and they know how to work with others. . . .These students are both challenging and exhilarating to teach" (Joyce et al., 2004, p. 9). Teachers must learn to teach experientially and trust students to become involved with these kinds of interactive learning (Steinaker, 2007b). In order

STANDARDS AND CREATIVE PLANNING   13

to ensure that motivation and creativity occurred in planning, teachers must

not only trust students but must "authentically commit themselves [and]

examine themselves constantly" (Freire, 2006, p. 60). "Professional teaching

is a process of giving and receiving, of sharing and listening, and of visioning

and achieving. Creativity and challenge are the underpinnings of these

dimensions of professional teaching" (Steinaker, 2006b, p. 2).

Reeves has noted, "teachers who create effective standards-based

performance assignments are the heroes of education" (2004, p. 140).

Every teacher has become a leader and every student has shared in that

leadership. "Leadership is a passionate exercise toward the implementation

of a personal and a shared vision" (Steinaker, 2005, p. 1).

"Synectics [creativity] is used to help us develop fresh ways of thinking

about the student, the student's motives, the nature of penalties, our goals,

and the nature of the problem" (Joyce et al., 2004, p. 163). Standards-based

planning has been an essential incentive toward creativity and interactive

teaching (Steinaker, 2006a). A student who said education is not a

destination, but is a journey that continues in the hearts and minds of

teachers who love and care for their students' best stated this perspective. May

we all begin that journey with continuity, commitment, courage, community,

and compassion. May we engage students in dialogue and direction so that

they may find purpose and continue their personal Journey positively and

with integrity (Steinaker, 2006a, p. 3).

Discussion

Summary

Standards have "become a major policy vehicle" (Darling-Hammond 2001, p. 211) Personnel in every state have developed standards or performance descriptors (Reeves, 2004). Darling-Hammond (2001) saw the use of standards as a means of reform or transformation of the schools. She also suggested that there should be fewer standards and more in depth learning. It was noted that learning should be an experience which students could internalize (Steinaker & Bell, 1979). When teachers planned lessons the "how of teaching becomes more important than what we teach" (Steinaker, 2006b, p. 2). Standards are not new to American education. As early as 1924, Bobbitt suggested more than 800 goals for students. Ornstein and Hunkins (2004) noted that students in an information age must "meet higher demands on their levels of knowledge and skills" (p. 393). This required a "carefully structured curriculum and instructional program" (Steinaker & Harrison, 1976, pp. 75-76). Bruner (1959) felt that learning involved organized experiences, which could be transferred. Dewey (1910) called this reflective thinking. Serdyukov (2004) called lesson planning "essential" (p. 5). A major problem in performance-based instruction has been resources (North Central, 2006). HELP has been one such resource. It was a lesson-planning format which was

STANDARDS AND CREATIVE PLANNING   15

professional in structure and purpose and which allowed for creativity and

in depth learning (Steinaker 2006b). Within this program, using links to

professional documentation, support was immediately available to

teachers. Steinaker & Bell (1979) defined creativity as having five

sequential steps. They suggested that teachers use creative learning

experiences, which involve students in planning. Further it was noted that

motivation and creativity occur in planning when teachers "authentically

commit themselves" to teaching (Freire, 2006, p. 60). Joyce et al. (2004)

called these involved students "challenging and exhilarating to teach"

(p. 9). Steinaker (2007b) noted this as interactive learning. Finally it was

suggested by Steinaker (2006b) that standards-based planning was an

incentive toward creativity and interactive teaching.

Interpretation

Standards are not new to American education. I agree with

Ornstein & Hunkins (2004) that they have been with us from the twenties.

Since all states have standards or performance descriptors (Reeves, 2004),

I believe, with Serdyukov (2004) that careful planning and instruction are

essential to student learning. I further believe that the effective use of

standards can reform or even bring about transformation in schools

(Darling-Hammond, 2001). I also concur with authors at North Central

Regional Educational Laboratory (2006) that one of the major issues in

STANDARDS AND CREATIVE PLANNING   16

standards-based instructional programs is resources. Central to this issue

is that teachers and schools are "becoming increasingly accountable for

results (p. 1). Steinaker and Harrison (1976) posited that careful planning

is the most important factor in student achievement. I concur with this

view. HELP (Steinaker, 2007a) is one such resource for teachers in terms

of creative lesson planning. I believe that this program can become a

professional resource for teachers and schools. I also agree with Joyce

et al. (2004) that teachers can link each model of teaching to student

performance and student achievement of performance based standards.

   Reflective teaching (Dewey, 1910), transfer learning (Bruner, 1961)

and reciprocal teaching (Brown & Palinscar, 1989) are also ways of

defining interactive teaching, learning, and evaluation. I agree with

Steinaker and Bell (1979) that creativity can be defined and has five

observable steps. This creative teaching requires commitment on the part

of teachers (Freire, 2006) and creative planning and instruction to

"develop fresh ways of thinking (Joyce et al., 2004). Finally, I agree with

Steinaker (2006a) that standards-based planning, instruction, and

evaluation are strong incentives toward creativity and interactive teaching

and that "education is not a destination, but is a journey that continues in

the hearts and minds of teachers who love and care for their students"

(Steinaker, 2006a).

Conclusions and Recommendations

Based on the review of literature and on my interpretation of the literature reviewed, I have concluded that the effective use of standards-based planning and instruction can result in creative teaching and augmented student learning. I have also concluded that there are programs such as HELP, which can become an incentive to creative planning and teaching. Finally, I have concluded that in every lesson students must reach at least the application level of cognition.

Based on the review of literature, my interpretation, and conclusions, I recommend that teachers receive professional development on creative planning and implementation of standards. I further recommend that teachers use programs such as HELP as the format for their planning.

References

Brown, A., & Palinscar, A. (1989). Guided cooperative learning, individual knowledge acquisition. In L. Resnick (Ed.). *Knowing, learning, and instruction* (pp. 393-451). Hillsdale, NJ: Erlbaum.

Bruner, J. (1961). *The process of education.* Cambridge, MA: Harvard University Press.

California State Department of Education. (n.d.). *Content standards.* Retrieved from http://www.cde.ca.gov./be/st/ss-12k

Darling-Hammond, L. (2001). *The right to learn: A blueprint for creating schools that work.* San Francisco, CA: Jossey-Bass.

Dewey, J. (1910). *How we think.* Boston, MA: Heath.

Education World. (2006). National and state standards. http://www.education-world.com/standards/state/index.shtml

Freire, P. (2006). *Pedagogy of the oppressed.* New York, NY: The Continuum International Publishing Group, Inc.

Joyce, B., Weil, M., with Calhoun, E. (2004). *Models of teaching* (7th ed.). Boston, MA: Pearson Education, Inc.

North Central Regional Educational Laboratory. (2006). Critical issue: Rethinking the use of educational resources to support higher student achievement. Retrieved from http://www.ncrel.org/sdrs/areas/issues/envirnmnt/go/go600.htm

Ornstein, A. C., & Hunkins, F. P. (2004). *Curriculum foundations, principles, and issues* (4th ed.). Boston, MA: Pearson Education, Inc.

STANDARDS AND CREATIVE PLANNING   19

Prisoners of time: The report of the national education commission on time and learning. (1994). Washington, DC: United States Printing Office.

Reeves, D. B. (2004). *Making standards work: How to implement standards-based assessment in the classroom, school, and district*. Denver, CO: Advanced Learning Press.

Serdyukov, P. (2004). *Effective lesson planning*. Boston, MA: Pearson Custom Publishers.

Shulman, L. (1983). Autonomy and obligation. In L. Shulman & G. Sykes (Eds.), *Handbook of teaching and policy* (pp. 484-504). White Plains, NY: Longman.

Steinaker, N. W. (2005). *Leadership*. Unpublished manuscript, National University.

Steinaker, N. W. (2006a). *Critical pedagogy: A perspective*. Unpublished manuscript, National University.

Steinaker, N. W. (2006b). *Using standards for professional planning*. Unpublished manuscript, National University.

Steinaker, N. W. (2007a). *Heuristic electronic lesson planner*. Trabuco Canyon, CA: Communications L.T.D.

Steinaker, N. W. (2007b). Standards as incentives for creativity. Trabuco Canyon, CA: Communications L.T.D.

Steinaker, N. W., & Bell, M. R. (1979). *The experiential taxonomy: A new approach to teaching and learning*. New York, NY: Academic Press.

Steinaker, N. W., & Harrison, M. (1976). *Measuring experiences through the experiential taxonomy.* Ontario, CA: Ontario-Montclair School District.

Steinaker, N. W., & Leavitt, L. (2007). *Simulation: An adventure in learning.* Trabuco Canyon, CA: Communications L.T.D.